LLEWE
2007
WICCA
ALMANAC
A GUIDE TO PAGAN LIVING

Featuring

Parthena Black, Dallas Jennifer Cobb,
Raven Digitalis, Taylor Ellwood, Emely Flak,
Link, Luna, Lupa, Paniteowl,
Daniel Pharr, Jason Pitzl-Waters,
Diana Rajchel, Skyewolf, Tammy Sullivan,
Patricia Telesco, Aar Tiana,
Annie Wilder,
Lady Mandrake Windwillow

Llewellyn's 2007 Wicca Almanac

ISBN-13: 978-0-7387-0335-0
ISBN-10: 0-7387-0335-4

Printed in the United States of America on recycled paper.
Editor: Sharon Leah
Designer: Michael Fallon
Cover Designer: Gavin Dayton Duffy
Cover Images: © Eyewire; © Photodisc; © Artville

Interior Illustrations: Brian Raszka 8, 10, 13, 65, 66, 82, 84; Christiane Grauert 18, 21, 24, 198, 200, 239; Matt Kenyon 28, 33, 192, 195, 243, 249; Selina Alko 38, 42, 95, 96, 233; Sean Qualls 48, 53, 91, 93; Stephen Schildbach 58, 60, 111, 116, 214, 216; Angelo Pennacchio 72, 75, 76, 218, 221, 259, 262; Laurie Luczak 208, 210, 269, 272, 274; Terry Miura 100, 105, 224, 228; photo courtesy of Aar Tiana 79

Additional Clip Art Illustrations: © Digital Vision; © PhotoDisc; © Brand X; © Digital Stock; © Image 100. Models are used for illustrative purposes only and may not endorse or represent the books subject matter.

Special thanks to Amber Wolfe for the use of daily color correspondences. For more detailed information on this subject, please see *Personal Alchemy* by Amber Wolfe.

Any Internet references contained in this work are current at publication time, but the publisher cannot guarantee that a specific location will continue to be maintained.

You can order Llewellyn annuals and books from *New Worlds*, Llewellyn's magazine catalog. To request a free copy of the catalog, call toll-free 1-877-NEW-WRLD, or visit our Web site at http://subscriptions.llewellyn.com.

Astrological calculations were performed by the Kepler program by permission of Cosmic Patterns Software, Inc., (www.AstroSoftware.com)

Llewellyn Worldwide
Dept. 0-7387-0335-4
2143 Wooddale Drive
Woodbury, MN 55125-2989
www.llewellyn.com

Llewellyn's 2007 Wicca Almanac

Contents

Chapter Three: Sweep Me Away!

Tips & suggestions for Wiccans & Pagans who wander through the wide & wondrous world

Chapter Four: Over the Cauldron

Up-to-date Wiccan & Pagan opinions & rantings overheard & spelled out just for you

Chapter Five: Media Witch

The Witchy Wide Web, technology, & electronic magic

Introduction: From the Editor

Welcome, and thank you for pausing a moment to look at the latest edition of Llewellyn's *Wicca Almanac*. My appreciation for writers was renewed as this edition took shape. We chose our contributors because they were willing to share personal experiences and insights with you, and they really came through for us.

The *Wicca Almanac* embraces the do-it-yourself aesthetic and is geared to practitioners on various paths of the world's most ancient spiritual traditions. On the pages that follow, you'll find in-depth (sometimes opinionated) articles on Pagan and Wiccan lifestyles, the media, the pros and cons of solitary practices, and making connections with other Witch-minded folks in your communities, covens, and on the Internet. The articles are as bright, colorful, entertaining, thought provoking, mysterious, and heartwarming as a kaleidoscope.

Your first glimpse into this Witchy kaleidoscope comes from Diana Rajchel, as she guides us through "Magic in the City." Patricia Telesco offers travel tips in "Wiccans in the Fast Lane," and Jason Pitzl-Waters's article "Blog the Gods" may be just the inspiration you need to start your own blog. And, if you're intrigued by the spirit world, be sure to read Tammy Sullivan's article "Spills & Chills of Ghost Hunting."

We enjoy inviting new voices to join us, and this year there are several. They include Raven Digitalis, Luna, Taylor Ellwood, Lupa, Skyewolf, Aar Tiana, Link, Annie Wilder, and Lady Mandrake Windwillow. Luna shares her inspiring vision quest in "We Are All Right!," Ellwood reminds us about the importance of ritual in "Stay Connected Anywhere," and Link applies humor and insight to daily living in "By the Book." And, for your convenience, information about holidays, Moon signs and Full Moon dates and times, and color correspondences can be found the almanac section. I hope you enjoy this year's *Wicca Almanac*.

—Sharon Leah, editor

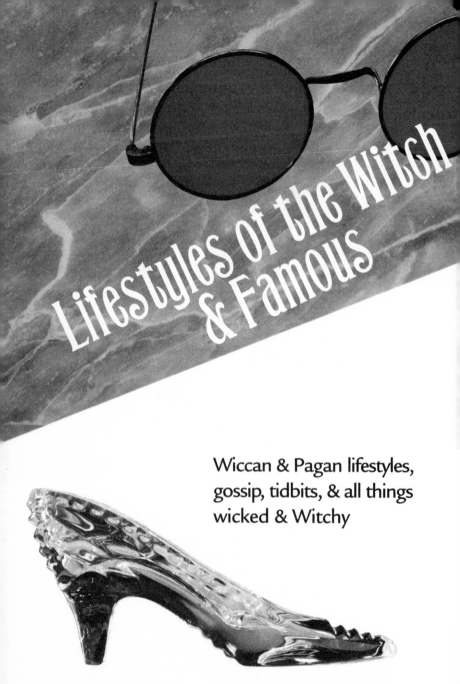

Lifestyles of the Witch & Famous

Wiccan & Pagan lifestyles, gossip, tidbits, & all things wicked & Witchy

Magic in the City
by Diana Rajchel

Urban magic, like any magic, requires the will to visualize and the desire to enact change. Urban centers, by virtue of having more people, can get more energy from those who become involved. To get people involved, you must harness their attention, and no one knows how to get attention quite like an artist.

My first experience with the possibility of ritual as performance art came from my favorite artist—Paul Rucker. A powerful visionary, and long active in Pagan and creative circles, he is deeply interested in ritual as theater. He took

ritual into places that didn't necessarily confront passers-by, but did challenge them. While he has yet to wander into the mainstream sphere, he is responsible for some of the most successful rituals I've seen within the Pagan community.

The trademark of his rituals was their tactile experiences. His rituals had drama, masks, and elaborate costuming. When dancers entered the circle on realistic deer's legs and re-enacted the descent myth, the audience members felt as though they themselves were sinking below the earth.

There was no space for passivity. These were powerful images standing still, and interacting with them forced a change within me. They were ritual and theater and performance at their best. None of his rituals happened in a remote location. They were all urban, all the time.

Rituals play out on urban spaces in more than a Wiccan context. Urban rituals can happen when a play, sculpture, artwork, musical performance, or even a routine happening delivers a spiritual experience. While magic effects change, ritual takes a step beyond change and instills a sense of connection to something more than the self.

Sometimes, dropping coins in the fare box on the bus just gets me where I'm going. Other times, dropping the coins really gets me *where I'm going* . . . and I know it when I feel it.

Much like giving the coin to the boatman on the River Styx, dropping coins in the bus slot can move my experience from the daily grind to a series of synchronicities. Some days a runic inscription on the sidewalk that is meant to make passers-by happier means nothing. Other days people will pause, puzzle, and smile at the inscriptions.

People of the Street

I pass unconscious priests of a city wandering the streets, chattering about the history of buildings or trying to bum a cigarette off of someone, unaware that they are creating a moving myth of the city around them with each encounter they have with another person. Buskers bring music and a mood to busy byways; and most are not homeless and desperate, but play in other venues, too. For some, their street performances are a rite of passage as they "earn their chops" in the sometimes hostile environment of street performance.

Street Theater

Street theater is a time-honored tradition. These spontaneous, small dramas are performed as audiences walk past. Dance always evokes a strong reaction when it happens in public. In the 1980s, people would gather on sidewalks with a boom box and perform break-dances. While some cities banned dancing in the streets, the bans are being lifted and hopefully such performances will return. Dancing has always been

Public sculptures make strong magical focal points; the Statue of Liberty has infinite possibilities because of its iconic nature.

a way of raising energy in ritual and magical practice. Shamans performed dances to bring rain and fertility, and Bible accounts tell of dances performed to praise God. Dancing in the street

sometimes brings money; it can bring a moment's happiness, or relief from the press of brick and stone that's all around us.

Public Sculpture

Public sculpture is another example of art in the urban setting. Whether grandiose statues of historical figures or pop-culture celebrations, these structures create both a focal point and an iconography for people to enjoy.

There are many icons in Washington D.C. for the people to identify with; the Washington Monument, the Lincoln Memorial, and the Vietnam Veterans Memorial Wall are all powerful images we share in our collective consciousness. That these images send such powerful messages is evidence of their power and their usefulness in a magical context. Each monument can be an anchor for magical working by any number of people.

Public sculptures make strong magical focal points. A friend of mine used the Mary Tyler Moore statue in downtown Minneapolis as a center for a spell to make her a stronger single woman. People who want to hold peacemaking conversations visit the cement buffalo that was installed in Mankato, Minnesota, as a gesture of apology to indigenous people. It is believed that the buffalo spirit it represents encourages healing and reconciliation.

The Statue of Liberty has infinite possibilities because of its iconic nature. Someone who wants to project peace, liberty, and protection could perform a ritual from a space where they could see her, and visualize rays of liberty and freedom shooting out from her torch. It isn't even necessary to be in New York to do this, although that location might make the intention stronger.

Graffiti

Along with grand monuments and large-scale sculpture, an expression of the common people—graffiti—can be an art form, too. Whether or not graffiti is "art" or vandalism depends on whether or not the tagger (graffiti artist) follows a code of honor. As with occultists, dabblers are distinguished from true adepts by their awareness and honoring of such codes. Graffiti artists restrict "tags" (pieces of graffiti art) to public structures, such as highway overpasses and bus shelters. None would tag a residence, and most would keep business tagging to the alleys and backs of buildings. Those who tag business windows and homes are viewed as amateurish vandals.

Graffiti artists who tag improbable spots also earn a place of honor for the courage and/or insanity required to climb up on some buildings and overpasses to make these marks. The graffiti tags either make a structure more beautiful or they send a powerful message through sparse comments or sharp images.

In Minneapolis, graffiti artists make the sharpest public comments. After one eminent domain dispute, someone saw fit to spray "sold" on a heavily traveled underpass. Near a bridge leading to the University of Minnesota, one tagger sprayed jokes in mathematical symbols.

Street Evangelists

Possibly less appreciated, but more recognized among urban artists, are the street evangelists. These icons of a bygone era use polished public speeches as powerful tools of movement and change. While the messages the evangelists bring are often obnoxious and offensive, what they do takes skill and practice, and their performances are motivated by their own spiritual needs. These street preachers put on powerful performances, and do what many a Wiccan priest or priestess attempts in ritual; they use words and motion to incite emotional reactions.

Groups that gather to engage in life-building activities can make it possible to reclaim public spaces . . .

While preaching the gospel of Wicca would make for unneeded embarrassment among Wiccans, a powerful speaker can use the skills of public speech to read poems about everyday beauty without turning into yet another evangelist. Urban art and public performance reach beyond the works of individuals. Whether someone reads Shakespeare in the park or a band spontaneously rehearses on the corner of a residential block, organized efforts attract an audience and they can stimulate a deep degree of change. (Finding artists who will organize and work in groups can be miraculous magic in itself!)

Cities are thriving sources of energy and creative thought, but perhaps the greatest gift of an urban environment is anonymity. But, like any magical tool, anonymity can be double-edged. On the days you don't want to talk to anyone, you can get exactly what you want, even when surrounded by people. Conversely, corruption, racism, and divisions happen because, in part, people don't talk to each other. And when they do talk, it's more about getting what they can from the other person than building community and relationships.

Get Involved

Ritual art in groups can have a potent place in resolving some issues of city living. If enough people are courageous enough to act silly in public, things can be done to influence others to rethink their daily routines and really look at where they're living—and, perhaps, to do something about it.

It's easy to stage a performance and alter a mood or promote a specific energy in an area with music. Drum jams are particularly effective for this purpose. Miami Beach in Florida has a Full Moon drum jam that draws people from all over for dancing, drumming, and a good time on warm nights. The performances create a sense of community and a safe space in what is often a crime-ridden area. A permit may be required, and there's a chance passers-by will think the performers are crazy, but with invention and a few companions, it's possible to set up an interesting performance.

The city belongs to those who live in it, and living in a city makes you responsible for it.

A Pagan Legacy

Pagan tradition has left a legacy of Paganism-related plays in the public domain, and you can look into Greek plays for some of the earliest plays. You might consider adapting one of them to street theater.

Spaces for Ritual

Most Wiccans think worship should happen outdoors, and urban magicals naturally head to public parks. Given the limited space of a city, it makes sense to go to places set aside as open space. City parks can also allow for trend adaptations. For instance, people can gather in a park for "cosplay" (costume play) and the characters can create an imaginative space for a desired change—a safer neighborhood or raising the activist spirit of a place. People can dress as the city's historical figures, or personify an element of the geography such as a river or island.

Because parks are gathering places for rest and socialization, they can also be subverted for negative activities. A park in Minneapolis has been damaged by gang activity, and cemeteries can be unsafe at night in New Orleans for the same reason. Groups that gather to engage in life-building activities can make it possible to reclaim these spaces, though. While playing in a park helps, working in it helps more. The best way to take back a park or public space is to clean it. Litter clean-ups and neighborhood watches tell any criminal element to back away as you take ownership of your land and space.

The city belongs to those who live in it, and living in a city makes you responsible for it. Yes, you elect officials and pay taxes for police officers and public transportation, but that's only a small part of a citizen's responsibility. So long as you live in a city, you are its creator and its guardian, and you are an artist. You can use your magic to make it change. Cities have power and spirit within them that is waiting to be tapped.

A Crowd of Solitaries

by Lupa

Wolves run in packs. Geese fly in flocks. Horses travel in herds. Witches work in covens. Right? Well, sometimes they do.

While the prevailing image people have of witchcraft is of coven members working together, and the earliest Wiccans believed you had to trace your lineage to Gerald Gardner to be considered legitimate, these days more and more Wiccans and Pagans are solitary practitioners.

This trend is particularly strong among those of us in the thirty and under crowd. We often spend more of our time as solitaries than in working groups. Many of us even prefer working alone. This is a far cry from the Wicca of fifty years ago, when all rituals were designed for covens and resources for solitaries were still decades away.

So why is there such a great disparity between then and now? After all, the advent of the Internet has made it simpler than ever to organize a group. Just a few mouse-clicks and you can get in touch with any of a number of people in your area who are ready and willing to practice magic together and trade notes. And with the increase of public rituals offered both by individual groups and at events such as Pagan Pride Day, anyone who shows up can make connections with others, and get a taste of group work.

Resources Abound

Part of the reason there are so many solitaries today is that those of us who are thirty-and-under have had access to a lot more resources. We have a lot to thank Scott Cunningham for, too. He introduced the idea of Wicca as a solitary path through his writings, which allowed a lot more freedom for individual expression, and, eventually, to the publication of more (and varied) books. Older Pagans had only a few books and magazines to choose from, and many times they had to remain completely hidden, which lessened the chances of ever meeting those of a like mind. We, on the other hand, can go to any bookstore and within a few minutes find something we like. And safe opportunities to meet other Pagans abound.

The Internet resulted in an information explosion beyond anyone's imagination.

The increasing variety of traditions and paths available is another reason for people to choose a solitary path. Druidry,

Asatru, Celtic reconstructionism, chaos magic, and literally hundreds of other paths have joined Wicca. In addition, ceremonial magical paths that predate Wicca still enjoy a healthy membership.

We Can Choose Our Own Path

If there's no one tradition you agree with, it's perfectly acceptable these days to create your own. If you don't like what's out there, it's a common practice to pull a Martin Luther—just pound your ninety-five theses into the door of the nearest status quo—and go gather the people who agree with you and start your own sect. Wicca is an excellent example of this kind of autonomy. Dozens of traditions have sprouted off of previous ones, with many made up only of a single coven that disagreed with the parent traditions' parameters.

The magical partnership is a very flexible way to bounce ideas in both theory and practice off of another person.

The proportion of followers to leaders is large, too, thanks to the increasing number of people introduced to Pagan religions through books and the Internet. Many covens choose to work privately because they don't want to be inundated with would-be members, many of whom want to convince the already-established coven why they would be an asset rather than an intrusion into their rather formal, intimate dynamic. The same goes for individual teachers who prefer to handpick their students rather than teach just anyone who comes along.

This means that more often than not the introduction to group work is through informal groups, like discussion groups that only talk about magic and religion rather than practicing together. Informal groups tend to meet in a public place (such as a bookstore) and have a set topic every month. These meetings often serve more of a social than a spiritual purpose in the Pagan community. Occasionally, community-wide rituals will attempt to include all participants, but there are usually few primary roles and most people end up being mere spectators.

It's very common for three or four neophytes to meet semi-regularly without any experienced guidance, and the members don't necessarily all follow the same path. Danielle, an online acquaintance, describes her situation:

> I am part of a five-person working group, but it's nothing formal; we get together for sabbats, we learn from each other, we work energy together, but there's no formal write-up and no formal bonds. My specific path (Kemetism, a modern religion based upon the ancient Egyptian family of gods/goddesses and the concepts of Ma'at and Netjer) differs from everyone else's path in my group. No one really follows the same path. There's a Vedic Pagan, a Celtic/shaman/something, a Norse recon, a Christopagan, and me, the Kemetic.

Together these people go through their growing pains, until for reasons that range from circumstance to simply out-growing the group, the loosely knit group disbands.

Sometimes these informal groups try to become more formal. The results vary. Nick Farrell, in his book *Gathering the Magic: Creating 21st Century Esoteric Groups*, described a number of pitfalls experienced by new formal groups. They range from not putting enough effort into group formation, to becoming a cult that centers around one particularly loud ego, to being so unstructured in an attempt to be egalitarian that the group disintegrates.

Another common situation is finding a magical partner to work with, usually (though not always) on a short-term basis. The partnership is the supreme example of why group dynamics can be so difficult. Trying to get two people to agree on something for more than one or two rituals can seem next to impossible! Still, it's a popular working format, one that is often carried out with a significant other or close friend rather than a casual acquaintance.

You don't have to be limited to just one magical partnership, as Alice, a twenty-four-year-old chaos magician, describes:

> Almost everyone I'm friends with is a magician of some sort, so opportunities appear often. We usually coordinate on a single goal rather than work on a single ritual—choose something both/each of us wants done—and contribute to its completion independently in our own idiosyncratic way.

The magical partnership is a very flexible way to bounce ideas in both theory and practice off of another person. It increases the amount of effort put toward the goal, while allowing each person to be more or less independent.

In fact, there has been a strong pull toward autonomy in Paganism in recent years. Covens and other formal groups are much too structured for many Pagans, which leads to dissatisfaction with the standard procedures. Fox, a twenty-one-year-old who primarily follows his own "agnosto-pantheistic thing," spent a period of time with the Order of Bards, Ovates, and Druids, and from time to time he touches base with the local Pagan Student Alliance. However, he still prefers solitude:

> The PSA does formal rituals via the local Pagan church. Most of this is venerating the gods/goddess . . . Being (a) agnostic and (b) allergic to worshipping anything has left me not wanting to participate. I've been a loner for my entire life,

anyway. I get uncomfortable and bored with anything beyond actually doing something. My idea of "ritual" is cleaning off my altar, with no pomp and circumstance . . . and half the time it occurs spontaneously. I'd much rather go running around in the woods than stand in a circle, anyway.

I tend to agree with Fox. I started out in a small informal group of friends (none of whom, me included, had a single clue what we were doing). Over the years I did very little group work, and as time went by I developed my own opinions and views on how spirit and magic work. These days I'm to the point where I really don't want to work with anyone other than occasional single rituals with my partner, Taylor, or one of my few very close friends. I don't have the time to try to explain my world view to others effectively enough to be able to successfully pull off a rite of magic with them. In addition, the only reason I've ever really felt the need for group work has been to socialize, and now that I have a network of Pagan friends and acquaintances, I no longer feel the need to be in a group.

Still, there will always be those for whom solitary practice is more important, even while they acknowledge the benefits of group practice.

Still, some people prefer groups to solitary practice. The problem of isolation has never gone away, and books and online resources cannot replace the value of contact with people. So, when the opportunity to work with others arises, many Pagans do take it. Nick Farrell points out, too, that while solitary practice can get things done quicker, a group has more resources.

Dr. Philip A. Bernhardt-House is a thirty-something Celtic reconstructionist. He brings up a number of positive reasons to be in a group that echo the benefits of strength in numbers:

22

The group [Ecclesia Antinoi] I'm with now (as one of the organizers/focalizers!) has been my full-time religion/identification since 2002, because I was looking specifically for something more organized and communal; solitary practice no longer appealed to me, I wanted shared experience and ideas and people to do ritual with rather than only having intellectual discussions with other pagans who may or may not agree with me on major and minor issues. Also, having accountability and a reality check from others, and regular holidays and such, gave the whole thing a lot more structure and, for lack of a better term, "realism" or authenticity than being solitary (which I think is, for many people I met and including myself, about one degree off of "non-practicing pagan" a good deal of the time).

Being part of a coven or other group doesn't necessarily negate the need for solitary practice. Dawa Lhamo, twenty-three, was raised in a Wiccan household and so has always had the opportunity for group interaction and practice. However, there's always time alone:

Well, people in groups tend to also work their own personal rituals solitary. It's not an either/or, really. Coveners do the group thing and the solitary thing, while solitaries do everything alone. We don't meet as a coven for daily ritual or for every little thing . . . The coven I visit meets weekly, and my regular coven meets at esbats, and the council meets at sabbats . . . I remain a Witch through the interim. Therefore, I do what needs to be done by myself in that space. One has to stand on one's own before one can really stand with a group.

Still, there will always be those for whom solitary practice is more important, even while they acknowledge the benefits of

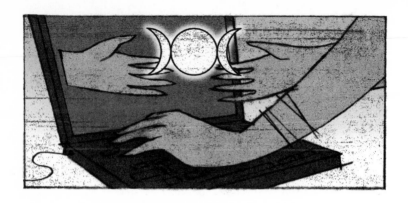

group practice. Nicholas Graham drew a lot of information for his book *The Four Powers* from his solitary work during his teens and early twenties. While he delved into numerous paths, he has only recently begun working with formal groups—an Alexandrian coven and a Rosicrucian Order. He says:

> I will never give up my solitary practice. I think that when you come right down to it, magic of any sort is a solitary path. Group work can be helpful, educational and extremely fun, but it can never be any more than a supplement. The Order with which I am involved is mostly a training and initiatory Order, not a working group. The coven is a teaching, initiatory and working group on the purely magical level, but is also a social/family group for those who fit in and are willing to devote themselves. The teaching is nice, well-energized initiation rituals can be extremely helpful, and group magic can be fun, but none of it is truly necessary.

In the end, the decision to join a group, or not, is an individual one. If you do decide you want to join a group, there are plenty of online resources, the most comprehensive being http//www.witchvox.com (specifically, the Witches of the World section). There are plenty of Web sites, forums, and listservs dedicated to regional and local Pagan groups and communities, and to advertising Pagan events. There are even books written about Pagan group dynamics. A good example is Nick Farrell's *Gathering the Magic*, which explores a number of different types of Pagan groups, not just the coven.

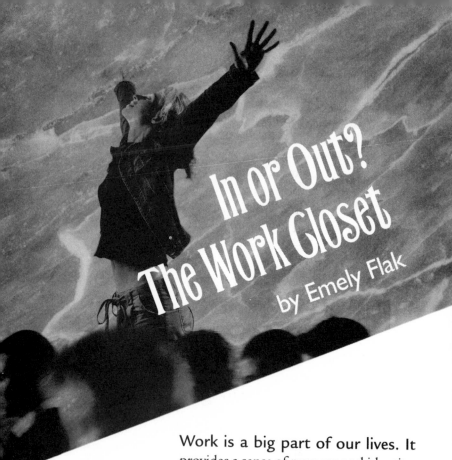

In or Out? The Work Closet

by Emely Flak

Work is a big part of our lives. It provides a sense of purpose and identity, and it carries financial rewards. Often, we spend more hours at work than with our friends and family, and the workplace becomes part of our community. In this community, where we encounter positive and negative experiences, it's important to feel comfortable with who we are. As priorities and conditions in the workplace shift, many people want to find an employer or occupation that matches their values.

Today, globalism and technology, management and motivation of people, and interpersonal skills—the ability to navigate social communications—are high priorities for companies and employees. We want our work to be more integrated into our lives, and we want our personal values to be aligned with those of our employer. Work environments that value competitive and aggressive behavior are being replaced by companies that reward integrity, ethical behavior, spiritual values, and well-developed interpersonal skills. Work and life balance is an often-discussed topic, and progressive organizations provide wellness programs such as yoga and meditation classes for their employees.

Remember that your passion may be their poison . . . never evangelize.

At one time, some people believed one couldn't be spiritual *and* be successful in business. Today, more companies strive to be known as "organizations with soul" or "socially responsible," because they want to attract (and keep) talented employees. When an organization combines its focus on profitability with strategies that support environmental sustainability, social responsibility, and global harmony, it has a better chance of earning the reputation for being an organization with spirit. The employees of companies with spirit have more opportunity to be who they are at work and to achieve professional advancement.

If you are unsure of your own values, ask yourself: What do I stand for? What will I not stand for? As more companies see an increase in their employees' social conscience, they will also recognize the importance of demonstrating their commitment to corporate social responsibility. With our personal and professional lives better integrated, more people want to work in companies with values that match their own.

Coming Out

One might argue that the time is right for Pagans and Wiccans to come out of the broom closet without fear. However, before you broadcast your magical ways to your colleagues, carefully consider the pros and cons. Although religious choice is a protected attribute, it is difficult to prove some workplace discrimination, and you risk being misunderstood. So, if you do come out of the broom closet, what can you expect?

> **"There's no such thing as Witches, just like there are no fairies!"**

Some Things to Think About

It is possible to be who you are at work without disclosing details about your spiritual preferences, but if you decide to come out, consider your coworkers level of tolerance and awareness of diversity. Have your colleagues had previous exposure to other alternative practices, Witches, or Pagans? Also consider possible consequences of too much interest, unrealistic expectations, disbelief, or hostility. It is likely that what they know about Wicca is inaccurate.

If you decide to reveal your spiritual practices, take precautions. It's easy to assume that once you start talking about your spiritual passion, others will be equally enthusiastic. Remember that your passion may be their poison, so never evangelize. Not preaching or trying to convert is an important aspect of Wicca.

Some Things to Expect

Expect to encounter questions and be prepared with answers. Consider questions as opportunities for you to educate others about Wicca. Here are some typical questions you may be asked: Do you believe in God? What are your main beliefs? Where do you go to pray? Is Wicca just for women? Is Wicca anti-Christian, or Satan worship? Are Witches naked during rituals? Do Witches perform sex rituals?

You can expect to be asked for help. Some people with unrealistic expectations may ask for help and expect you to dispense magic to cure their problems. A Wiccan friend told me she regretted discussing her Pagan path when a manager asked for a spell to help her daughter study for a school exam. A couple of days later the manager accused my friend of supplying ineffective spells because her daughter had found the exam difficult. My friend could only reply that spells did not come with guarantees. In these situations, it can be complicated to explain the ethics and variables of magic, and that the deities interpret intention and apply what is "for the good of all."

Sharing information about your lifestyle at work can promote witchcraft as a positive and credible path.

One Witch who came out of the closet at work told me that she wasn't ostracized. Instead, female colleagues wanted to talk to her all day, which became a distraction. You too may attract unwanted attention, including scrutiny from your manager.

You can expect that some people will have unrealistic expectations. You may hear comments such as: "If you are a Witch, then tell me the lotto numbers," or "If your spells are good, can you make me rich?" Sometimes, people will come to you for spells to get even with their tormentors. In these situations, you are bound to explain the basic principles of responsible magic and ethical practices.

You can expect people's disbelief. Remember that everyone does not regard Wicca as a credible spiritual path, and people you least expect it of can be the source of disbelief. A well-informed colleague mentioned to me, over a cup of coffee, that she had read an article about a recent census that reported an increased number of people who listed Wicca as a religion. A second colleague overheard our conversation and asked what Wicca was. My learned colleague briefly explained that it is the practice of witchcraft and mentioned I was Wiccan. My less-informed coworker laughed loudly and said, "You are so funny Emely. There is no such thing as Witches, just like there are no fairies." It is a daunting prospect for some people to consider working alongside a Witch.

The least desirable response to disclosing your Wiccan ways at work is hostility and the "silent treatment." (As mentioned earlier, discrimination can be difficult to prove.) If your disclosure will limit opportunities for promotion or selection for work-based projects, you need to carefully assess the risk and consequences of disclosure.

On a Positive Note

Sharing information about your lifestyle at work can promote witchcraft as a positive and credible path. You could find other like-minded individuals and create an interest in what you do, while also building trust with others and growing friendships. But, there is nothing wrong with remaining silent about your Wiccan path. Only you can decide if it is the right time.

Spiritual Expression at Work

The word "spirituality" has various definitions and perspectives. Spirituality can mean something as simple as a discussion about personal values, human motivation, and the meaning of happiness and job satisfaction. Sometimes benefits, like stress release and team building, result from these non-religious discussions. (Wicca provides a sound framework to help you deal with the conflict and power games that pervade the work environment.)

When does spirituality at work become too much? It's probably too much when discussion becomes religion-focused or self-centered. Be careful of pushing boundaries. If you start talking about Wicca incessantly, you risk annoying colleagues and being branded a "Bible-basher."

Personal Protection

Despite already-mentioned changes in the workplace and the increased demand for ethical behavior and socially sound policies, there are times when you need to protect yourself from negative energies and difficult people.

A challenging situation can occur quickly, and you need to call upon quick magic for your immediate protection. When there's no time to collect ritual tools, write spells, and wait for the right Moon phase, don't underestimate the power of visualization. Remember that all the resources you need are in your mind. Below are three simple visualizations that have proven to be extremely effective.

Protective Light or Bubble

In your mind's eye, imagine a protective shield of soft white light around you, like a bubble. On the out breath, imagine you are releasing gray, toxic energy. On the in breath, imagine you are breathing in white, pure energy that is reinforcing your protective shield. Slowly breathe in and out. Recharge your protective shield throughout the day.

Your personal objects remind you of work/life balance and the importance of inner calm and stress release.

Mirror

When approached by difficult people, imagine you are holding up a mirror to deflect their intent and energy, and watch their energy return to them. This strategy is particularly effective because it also gives you a few moments to consider your response. Say to yourself: *All the energy you send to me*

will be returned to you times three. If you need to perform this type of contingency magic, repeat the words like a mantra to raise the energy.

Spiritual Guardian

A spiritual guardian is useful when you anticipate a difficult meeting or potential conflict. When I face potential disagreement and conflict, I imagine the goddess Athena is with me in the office. Athena, with her owl on her shoulder, helps me to understand comments that would normally make me feel defensive, and I look to her for guidance and support. She helps me maintain my emotional balance.

A friend of mine created a "secret altar" collage on a letter-size piece of paper with photos to represent the four elements.

You don't need to wait for a difficult encounter to appoint a spiritual guardian. Take one with you everywhere. Change your guardian to suit the situation. Allow them to protect you, and empower them with your trust.

"Altar" Your Work Space

If your work environment is not entirely soothing, don't despair. Small changes can be made in your work area or office that will impact your surroundings. Whether or not you have announced your interest in witchcraft, you can create sacred space in your office or at your workstation. You don't need to set up a full altar. Instead, surround yourself with items that remind you of the natural world and your spiritual self.

Personalizing your workstation or office will nourish your spiritual essence and provide visual and auditory messages that are unique to you, that minimize stress and give you a source of focus and inspiration. Look around your office and take note of any natural elements you see. Remove dried flowers

When you "altar" your work area, you create and protect your sacred space and make your workspace individual to you.

and plants because they drain energy and affect the visual impact of your workspace. Bring in plants, flowers, and moving water (first, check if water features are allowed) to create energy flow and bring the natural environment to you. Make sure your plants are free of dust. If using real items is not possible, try a photograph, a shell, or a rock.

A friend of mine created a "secret altar" collage on a letter-size piece of paper with photos to represent the four elements. She arranged images of the ocean, a cave, rock formations, clouds, and a spectacular sunset as four elements on an altar in cardinal directions. This paper representation of nature helped her stay connected with her Pagan path throughout the day.

When you "altar" your work area, you create and protect your sacred space and make your workspace individual to you. It becomes a place where you can relax and experience inner calm. Your personal objects remind you of work/life balance and the importance of inner calm and stress release.

Music

Listen to music, if you can. Music has a positive effect on your state of mind and well-being. It's been proven that music has properties to heal, soothe, and maximize mental function. Consider it a form of therapy.

It's easier to listen to music if you have your own office. Otherwise, listen to your favorite tunes on an iPod or MP3 player, and change the music to suit your mood or needs. On some days, I crave upbeat, energizing music; at other times, when I am in a more contemplative mood, I choose slower, calming music. Listen to music on the way to and from work, too.

Without necessarily disclosing details of your Wiccan path, you can express your spirituality in your workplace; and, you can work for an employer or company that demonstrates ethics and values in line with your own. When you can combine these techniques, you are truly being "who you are" at work.

Beyond the Threshold: the Energy of Places

by Annie Wilder

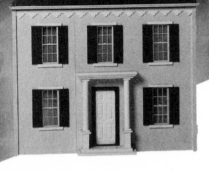

I'm home. I pull in the curving dirt driveway and park in front of the hundred-year-old outbuilding that is my garage. The garage was the lair of Leon Kuechenmeister, the old man who once owned my house. His energy signature is still palpable in the garage's dusty stillness. His thriftiness and sense of order are evident in the carefully stored trim boards, scrap lumber, and old rain gutters in the garage's attic rafters, and in the old fruit cans and baby food jars filled with nails, screws, and other hardware lined up neatly on home-made shelves. Whenever I run into trouble on a small repair project around my house, I ask Leon's spirit for help. Sometimes I hear a clearly spoken answer in my mind, sometimes I get an idea of a new approach to try. Occasionally, I don't sense any response at all, and every now and then, I just hear a chuckle.

The raspberry bushes I planted alongside the garage five or six years ago are loaded with ripe berries, ready to be picked and eaten fresh or made into sweet freezer jam. This spring, two visiting psychics told me they tuned into the capable and content energy of an old woman in my summer kitchen. She was washing the raspberries that her grandkids picked from the back yard; I wonder if the old woman's experience from decades ago influenced my decision to put in a raspberry patch.

Heading to my house, I walk past three pine trees that form a natural privacy screen on the west side of my back yard. I call them "the sisters" because their branches touch and it looks like they're holding hands. On the yard's east boulevard, tall Chinese elms, trees I was not happy to see when I first looked at my house, serve as sentries. Over the years, I've come to appreciate the old elms. They are the only trees in my yard big enough to

I believe that living in this house has helped to awaken my soul.

attract the crows that I find so interesting. I planted clematis around the elms' trunks and the trees seem more patient than I am at how long it's taking the capricious flowers to flourish. In the last few years, I've harvested morel mushrooms from my yard. My neighbor Wolf said that the mushrooms are a sign that the elm's root systems are dying. The mushrooms are yet another gift from the trees I thought I didn't want.

It's been twelve years since my kids and I moved into the grand but shabby hundred-year-old Victorian house in a historic Mississippi River town in Minnesota. From the beginning,

we felt the spirit of Leon Kuechenmeister. His watchful, brooding presence hung around the back of the house (which was where Leon lived after he converted the home into a triplex). It turned out that Leon had his reasons for sticking around the house. Some reasons involved important unfinished business, and others were a little more surprising.

When I bought the house, I knew there was a male ghost, but his energy didn't feel dangerous—just gloomy and heavy. I was enamored with the house's faded beauty, lost grandeur, and the stories and secrets I was certain it held. My kids were in high school, and I knew I was nearing the end of day-to-day parenting, which was a meaningful and important part of my life and a big part of my happiness. What my spirit needed was a wonderful old home that needed love and attention. I wanted a place that would inspire me and give me a new outlet for my creativity and energy. The old Victorian needed a lot of work, but I didn't mind. I figured I'd have the rest of my life to work on it. And I knew from experience that cleaning, beautifying, and repairing a home are all good ways to connect with it.

This old house taught me many things that I wouldn't have learned if I had lived somewhere else. One of the most dramatic effects that living here has had on me is that my intuitive and psychic abilities have increased. I think it's because this house is energetically unusual, and there are lots of odd happenings that have sharpened my awareness of the spirit realm. Shortly after we moved in, we discovered that Leon wasn't the only spirit living here. I started seeing the spirits of people who used to live here and seeing glimpses of the house as it used to be. I have seen old-fashioned spirit sisters who lived here in the late 1800s, and a sad woman who looks like she lived during the 1940s.

I believe that every place has a spirit and an identity of its own and that it is possible to work with its energy to create the kind of environment you want.

Over the years, my guests have experienced strange things, too. They've seen lights go off and on and doors slam shut by themselves. They've had weird dreams in which they thought they were awake, and heard heavy footsteps, laughter, and a man clearing his throat.

I've always thought of my house as having a feminine sensibility, and I knew how much fun and laughter and just plain energy my kids and I could bring to her. I think Leon's spirit needed peace and quiet and privacy. He hadn't spent any energy at all on the aesthetics of the home, although he was a master carpenter and kept the home structurally sound and in order. So, I believe that what my spirit needed was a better fit with the home's spirit or essential vibe. Once I started fixing up the house, I felt as though I was work-ing with my home's energy rather than against it, and that the spirit of the house was strengthened and reani-mated. And happy.

Recognizing the relation-ship we have with our living spaces opens up a lot of possibilities.

I believe every place has its own spirit and an identity, and that you can create the kind of environment you want when you work *with* that energy. It's easiest to do with your own space, like your home or apartment. If you have some space that you call your own, it's also possible to create an energetic haven at work.

After converting my house back to a single family home, completing most of the needed restoration work, and helping Leon take care of his unfinished business so he was no longer earthbound, my house's energy is mostly very cheery, warm, and inviting. My house looks loved and appreciated and it is.

I feel each of us is responsible for contributing to the energetic well-being of the planet, starting with ourselves and where we live. When my kids moved into their apartments, we washed windows, scrubbed and cleaned, and put in a few flowers in the places where it was possible to do so. Taking care of something is one of the best ways to show you value it. It establishes a positive connection with the spirit of the place and just adds to the general good vibe on all energetic levels.

When I moved into my house, except for the three Chinese elms on the boulevard and violet nightshade growing wild along the foundation, there were no trees, shrubs, vines, or flowers in the yard. I have added seventeen trees, a cotoneaster hedge around the back yard, lilacs, burning bushes, and a bunch of flower beds to add to the beauty and positive energy of my home. I did pay attention to the magical correspondences of many of the plants I brought into my yard. It's a good way to bring certain kinds of energy into your environment if you feel they are currently lacking. For example, I put in lots of daisies because they're friendly and I thought they were a good counterbalance to the nightshade. (I actually am very fond of nightshade, but I don't let it grow on my property because of its danger to children.)

Everything Is a Relationship

It comes down to a simple idea that is reinforced in belief systems from quantum physics to magical philosophy to simple etiquette: *everything is a relationship*. Recognizing the relationship we have with our living spaces opens up a lot of possibilities. It acknowledges the important role each of us plays in creating energetically healthy and positive places. It also provides a framework for starting to work with the energy of your living space, since each of us has participated in relationships of many varieties throughout our lives.

Along with seasonal rituals . . . perform blessing and protection rituals for your home and property, and cleansings after negative experiences.

So, where do you begin? The same way you'd start any relationship. Get to know your home. Get its story. Devote some of your magical energy and creativity to the process—it's a lot of fun. Tune in, pay attention, use intuition, ritual, dreamwork, meditation. Do research, talk to neighbors, visit your local historical society or library. Think about what was going on in your town, region, the country, and the world in the era in which your home was built. Material objects generally reflect the prevailing beliefs and mores of their time, and the people

who lived in your home before you were experiencing the events that to us, are stories from the past.

Here's how I see it. Any physical place is a convergence point and potential container for several different energies:

- Your spirit/your family's spirit.
- Any ghosts or astral beings attached to the space.
- Your home's spirit (by this I mean the energetic signature your home has accumulated over time from both physical and astral events and experiences).
- The spirit of the land.

This perspective recognizes the many levels of what's happening energy-wise in any particular space. It may seem daunting at first, but many levels of energy means there are many possibilities for connection and transformation. This perspective also provides a framework for cultivating positive energy through both magical and mundane practices. And remember, relationships develop over time—it's not possible (and not a good idea, either) to try to do everything at once. The stuff that's most important usually finds a way to get your attention. Since your energy will probably be the strongest vibe (unless you find yourself in a very energetically unusual place), that's a good place to begin.

Your Energetic Spaces

So, starting with your own spirit, ask yourself a few simple questions. (You can work your way through the questions below using any of the energetic perspectives listed above, i.e. house spirit, spirit of the land, and so on. Since they're all part of a big web of relationships, you'll find that they often overlap.)

- What does my spirit need?
- What does my spirit have to offer this place?
- What does the energy of this place have to offer me?
- What can I learn from the energy of this place?
- How can I be a good energy steward (which contributes to the energetic well being of both the physical and spirit worlds)?

My perspective on energy has developed over time and in an organic, trial and error sort of way. I have always had a hobbit nature and I have made my living cleaning houses at different times in my life so I'm particularly tuned into houses. I took an introductory shamanism course from Michael Harner and he said that once you have awakened your soul, you'll find that you get more vivid dreams because your soul knows you're listening to it.

Dreams: Connecting and Working With Subtle Energies

I believe that living in this house has helped to awaken my soul. I've always had cool dreams, but since moving in here, I've had lots of lucid dreams, and astral experiences as well. I've started bringing dream objects into my house as a way of honoring the importance of dream messages. I've found that if I encounter a particularly memorable object in a dream, such as a clock made of a giant mushroom cap or a photo album of my life with a lion on the cover, chances are good that I'll come across a similar object in my waking life.

In fact, I believe the message of the photo album dream was that I needed more adventure in my life. When I opened the photo album, it was empty. The woman at the store (which was in an airport) smiled and told me I needed to fill the album. When she told me it cost $35.00, I put it back on the shelf, telling her it was too expensive. I was thirty-five years old at the time. This dream resonated with me so much that I started an adventure theme in my living room. I got a globe, hung photographs of a magical old tree from Ireland, rigged up a toy airplane on a string that buzzes around in a circle, and displayed a papier-mâché sailboat made for me by my niece Gwendolyn. Shortly after having the dream I saw a gift wrap bag with a lion on it that looked like the photo album cover, so I bought it and have it where I see it everyday—on a desk near the mushroom cap "clock" I made. That's another way to cultivate positive energy in your living space, to make sure your dreams and hopes are part of your surroundings.

Other ways to be a good steward of the energy of your space include tuning into and honoring seasonal energy shifts through ritual and decorations. Besides developing your own energy-sensing skills, this is a good way to connect with the spirits of the land, since you are acknowledging the cadence and rhythm of the natural world they inhabit. Each season's energy offers its own gifts and opportunities. I've never appreciated winter the way I appreciate the other seasons, but now I view it as a good time for creative cocooning, which I need for my bigger writing projects and other artsy-type endeavors, like making fairy furniture and painting. I also use the inward focus of wintertime for indoor projects such as sorting through things and organizing rooms and closets.

Along with seasonal rituals, it's a good idea to perform blessing and protection rituals for your home and property, and cleansings after negative experiences. As part of the cleansing ritual, I reflect on the message or lesson to be learned from the negative experience. I think this perspective helps me both gain something and let go of the negativity more easily.

When we first experienced some of the haunting activity here, and after consulting a psychic, my kids and I performed our first blessing and protection ritual. We went through our house and blessed each doorway (which, in this big old house, is something like forty-nine doors). Since then, I have done a lot of energetic protection work in my home and of my property, using reiki, feng shui principles, prayer, and magic. Another psychic who visited my house this year walked into my bedroom and said she could feel the reiki energy, which I thought was very cool.

I feel I have a really strong relationship with my house and her spirit. The spirits of people who lived here before me who still stop by for visits, and I think I'm just now reaching the level of getting to know the land spirits.

My young nieces and nephews come to visit and I take them around the yard and share the stories with them—*These trees are the sisters. See, one of them is holding a robin's nest . . . Let's see if the raspberries bushes have any raspberries for us. Then we'll gather some twigs that the elm trees gave us to make fairy furniture . . .*

Rhythm for the Soul

by Patricia Telesco

Dance is the hidden language of the soul.

—Martha Graham

Since early in our human history, dance has been used to celebrate important moments and as an act of worship. People in New Guinea and many other places have believed that dance not only honors the divine, but that it makes weary spirits rejoice and puts dancers into communion with sacred energies. Some myths even say that without dance the movement of the universe itself would cease. The value of dance comes across very effectively in this New Guinea saying:

"The drum is never beaten uselessly. Dances are never merely useless!"

The soulful art of sacred dancing blends movement and mindfulness that any of us can use to improve our spiritual pursuits. We see all types of dance taking place in a wide variety of world faiths, including ecstatic dancing in the Charismatic churches, the Dance of Universal Peace in Unitarian churches, the Whirling Dervishes of Islam, the Sun Dance of the Lakota, and the ritualized dancing around a sacred fire at Neo-Pagan gatherings. All of these dancers honor movement as a means of connecting with Spirit and each other. And it's a way to better understand their place in the world. This sense of unity and awareness is exactly what sacred dance can be to each of us.

. . . release your expectations of what does or does not constitute sacred dance. It helps a great deal, as will being patient with yourself.

I suspect some of you may be thinking: "I have no rhythm!" or "I have two left feet!" Well, relax. Trust in the African proverb that says: "If you can walk, you can dance." I harbored similar uncertainties for a very long time. I have come to honor that truth, even though I was once terribly awkward. My parents worried that I'd run into something and do serious damage to myself. To help, they sent me to dance school. I never really excelled in any of the traditional forms of dance, but the joy of the dance filled every corner of my being. When the music played and my body moved, for a while it seemed that nothing else existed but the motion. In those moments I felt truly alive and whole.

For a while I lost sight of dance as an expressive tool. I got hung up on how other people perceived my movements. That is a normal response, but insecurity held me back for five years. It took the hands and heart of a good friend to gently

guide me out to a community circle and dance me around a few times. As we moved in a more purposeful way, it was easy to lose myself to the motion. We embraced the rhythm and flames as much as each other, and it was beautiful. That's exactly when I was struck with the sublime realization that what matters in sacred dance is you, your partner in dance, and the Divine. If the people gathered with you have their minds and hearts in the right place, they will not be looking at your feet (or their own, for that matter!). And what are you worried about if it's just you and the God or Goddess? Trust me when I say that she/he cares less about fancy footwork than the motivation of your spirit.

Whether or not you think that you have rhythm, or are coordinated and graceful, or had a dance class, I'm telling you that you can dance. I would even go further and say: if you can move any part of your body, you can dance. I have seen people in wheelchairs move their chairs with one hand and make images with the other to do some of the most beautiful dancing. Dance isn't limited to standing on two feet. Dancing is part of your spirit.

It's true that sacred dance is not the same as waltzing, or boogieing the night away at a jazz club. Your attitude toward the dance is key. Instead of just having fun, you're having mindful, purposeful fun. Not surprisingly, along with the resurgence of the drum as a ritual tool, people are also rediscovering the transformational power of dancing. (You'll have plenty of company on the dance floor.) Whether you choose to dance with the Goddess, dance to reclaim personal wholeness, or dance for world peace, the movement of your body's motion, spirit's song, and mind's focus become the medium for change. Dance releases something within us that helps us remember who we truly are and why we are here. It helps us to transform.

An Ancient Cadence

Any time you're thinking of integrating something, like sacred dance, into your Path, it's good to know where it came from, how it started, and how others utilized that tool effectively. So, let's back up for just a moment and look at the roots of sacred dance. While you might not think of dancing as a spiritual or magickal activity, historically speaking it certainly has been one. From an elderly Native American shaman to a young child growing up in New Guinea, people have danced in community rites and to commemorate our humanness and the ongoing rhythm of life.

Common people used dance to celebrate cycles, honor the land, ensure a successful hunt or battle, make crops grow and cattle fertile, to commemorate important moments between individuals, and to inspire friendship or courtship. Some dances marked passages at birth or death, and others venerated a god or goddess in the hope of receiving blessings. Some of these ritualized dances were based on local superstitions, and enacted with intent. For example:

- Sword dances in Tibet were believed to banish evil, while in Scotland similar dances were part of war rituals.
- European people danced around a tree on New Year's Day for luck, love, and prosperity in the new year.
- Greeks danced at the death of enemies to keep from being haunted.
- Saxons danced around the Yule log for well being, especially during the winter festivals.
- Nigerians dance at the end of the rainy season for good fortune and romance.

When reflecting upon these concepts, it's not surprising to discover that students of social history believe that dance was one of the first languages humans developed, hula being an excellent example. There's also pictorial evidence that as early as Neolithic times people were already using dance as a symbolic means of imploring the gods and raising energy. Later history seems to bear out this possibility since nearly every culture had special magickal dances. Etruscan dances, for example, were enacted to keep the celestial spheres moving as they should, while Egyptian line dances invoked the blessings of the Nile and its resident gods for fertile land. Greek Dionysian rituals danced to welcome their God and fertility, and Israelite prophets danced ecstatically to receive insight from the Divine. So, we certainly have a long and rich history to consider in putting together our ideas about sacred dance, and its role in our observances and worship.

Preparing in Mind and Body
Sacred dance is not performance; it's a prayer. It's a type of worship. It's a bridge between worlds, and a way to touch

not only your higher self, but the cosmos and the Divine. You become the center of a moving mandala, whose goal is to reach the center and then direct that energy positively. As with any magick, it's good to prepare yourself ahead of time.

When you enter a community fire circle, it helps to remember that the space is about a group (not just one individual). Even if you dance alone, releasing your expectations of what does or does not constitute sacred dance will help a great deal, as does being patient with yourself. It took years for some of your insecurities to build, so they're not likely to disappear overnight. Remember that in the context of sacred space, movements aren't about making an outward impression. Direct those efforts, instead, at inner energetic transformations that will flow outward of their own accord. Perhaps this is part of what Jesus alluded to in the Gnostic gospel of John when he said: "The universe belongs to the dancer. He who does not dance, does not know what happens." You may also find it helpful to pray or meditate before you dance, and while you're at it—stretch and hydrate! Wake up your body so your spirit can soar!

There is a unique, uninhibited spark created by dancing naked beneath a Full Moon with your god/goddess as a partner.

Finally, enter the sacred space slowly. Walk the ground, getting a feel for the surface beneath your feet. Listen carefully to the drums and extend your senses. What are they saying? What energy is being created here? Find your space in that forest of sound and movement and then fill it out. There is typically some sort of etiquette at many community circles, which may vary from region to region. Nonetheless, if you go into that space with honor, respect, and gratitude in your mind, heart, and feet—you can't go very far astray. Don't be afraid to ask other local dancers for insights and advice if you feel unsure.

Pattern or Freestyle, Costumes or Skyclad?

Some dancers move in a circle, others stand still. Some love to wear elaborate costumes that reflect a goal, others wear nothing at all. Each approach has merit, and should be considered for its symbolic and mental impact on your worship. For example, circle dances honor cycles and life's wheel. They're suited for things like community building and fertility. Dancing in a square accents earth energy, which is suitable for things like Gaia worship and opening the doorway for providence. Spiral dances wind "up" or "down" a specific type of energy. So if you're thinking of patterning out a dance, consider your goal and match it to the pattern you create.

The village shaman's use of costume is a fantastic example. The shaman's lavish costume includes a robe and mask to lend dramatic flair and to help him attune to the spirits being invoked. The villagers, rather than seeing the same man they knew by daylight, see a potent image that helps set the tone for the ritual ahead. That change in mental focus and ambiance can have great affect on the outcome of sacred dance. Clothing helps make the magick by putting everyone in the same frame of mind.

Then again, sometimes simplicity is sublime. There is a unique, uninhibited spark created by dancing naked beneath a Full Moon with your god/goddess as a partner. Everything of the mundane world remains behind (okay, except maybe bug repellent!). Just be wise in your choice of location.

Dances Around a Sacred Object

People have gathered around one central point—an altar, fire, stones—because that point holds meaning for the community. Dance that centers around a central point is a type of worship; it can consecrate and sanctify the object, and renew whatever is amiss (return water to the well or help plants grow, for example).

It's fun and liberating, and a kind of blessing, to dance around the house. Whenever I've moved into a new home I've often danced the land a few times as a letter of introduction, and to welcome my patrons/patronesses to that site. In fact, this is a good illustration of the "solo" dance—a private moment of worship, gratitude, and power-raising.

Shake It, Don't Break It

Whirling Dervishes are Sufi mystics who twirl in a circle to become one with God. Sufi dancing is enjoying a rebirth because it reveres both the Creator and creation. Modern variations on this dance illustrate a belief that consecrated movement will renew human awareness and continue the natural order. This, in turn, heals the Earth and the human spirit so we can move to the next level of enlightenment.

By comparison, Santerian dancers use their feet to draw *veves* (sacred symbols) as they dance to invoke various Beings. Sometimes the dancer is temporarily possessed by one of those Beings. This is considered a natural part of the relationship the dancer has with his or her Orisha.

Wiccan and Neo-Pagan versions of ecstatic dance varies widely from tradition to tradition, however it's safe to say that many (if not most) utilize the drum to aid in achieving a trance state. Drums are the heartbeat and part of humankind's tribal soul. Their beat somehow awakens that part of us that knows how to *be*, rather than to *think*.

Some people find it very easy to trance dance; others do not. I'm one of the latter. Nonetheless, that doesn't mean energy isn't moving. It's not necessary to trance to be an effective sacred dancer. Everyone has a place and purpose. I mention this because for a while I felt that I was doing something wrong. But in magick, as in life, "know thyself" is a great rule. It will come if you're meant to trance.

People who are in a trance when they dance should have a safe space (such as a drum crescent), then just let them be. Sudden interruptions can break the ecstatic moment and cause a very nasty headache, or confusion.

Seasonal and Situational Dances

If we look at the world's celebrations, there are an abundance of dances that honor a specific time of year or a set of circumstances. For example, Chinese, Celtic, and Australian people all have a dance for the dead. Bedouins had marital dances, as did Malaysians (who utilized henna as part of this ritual), and Native Americans still dance to invoke rain. These examples provide us with more food for thought as we consider how and when to integrate sacred dancing in our rites. Our ancestors weren't shy about bringing dance into nearly every occasion.

I think part of the reason we don't see as much dancing anymore has to do with the popularity of secular dance. That definitely has very different goals and creates a similarly different impact on the participants and viewers. It's sometimes hard for those of us brought up with that kind of dancing to switch gears, nonetheless it can be done. Attitude is everything!

Dance your prayers! Dance your thankfulness to the four corners of creation, and let the world dance with you.

Lords and Ladies of the Dance

There were many gods and goddesses around the world who presided over dance and movement, or who dancing invoked. For example, there's Shiva in Hindu tradition, whose dance defeats chaos and ignorance, but also causes earthquakes because of its exuberance! Shiva's lesson in my life has been about how I engage life's dance. I may choose my own steps and music and cause those "quakes," or mix them with the status quo for something less dramatic.

If you feel called to sacred dance, you may be attracted to one or more dance deities, too. Here are a few for your reference:

Syria: Baal Margod, lord of the dance

Etruscan: Corredoio, god of celebratory dance

Egypt: Hathor, goddess of dance and several other arts (Bast was also known to be worshipped in dance)

India: Holi, goddess of the dance

Polynesia: Hua-tini, god of dancing

Hawaii: Kapo, goddess of hula

Oruba: Oya, goddess of folk dances

Zuni: Pautiwa, god of ritual dances

Aztec: Ueuecoyotl, god of celebratory dance

When considering your approach to any of these Beings, it's polite to get to know them first. Learn to say their names correctly. Read about their myths and stories to understand cultural contexts and subtleties. Know how to honor them in your sacred dancing space. Then, begin to welcome them as dance partners.

The Last Steps

The journey of life is indeed a dance. There is no limit to how you can apply sacred dancing if you get creative. Dance your spells and charms! Dance your prayers! Dance your thankfulness to the four corners of creation, and let the world dance with you. The dance will change you, and you will change the dance. Dare to dream! Dare to dance!

Nature-Minded & Urban

by Dallas Jennifer Cobb

The news is full of scary stuff. Reports abound on the growing incidence of obesity, the prevalence of disease, and global warming. And then there are the advertisements for all the new stuff we "need" to buy. When overwhelmed by the news, I will retreat into nature to find peace, calm, and connection to Spirit. The outdoors helps me to be centered and feel good.

When we talk about getting grounded, we acknowledge how important nature is to our well-being. Nature, also important as a growth environment for our food and as an air purifier, can teach us a lot about

ourselves, magic, and the bigger cycles and energies at work in our lives. A connection to nature can help to balance us emotionally, connect us spiritually, and nurture us physically.

While I live in a rural area, and nature is right outside my door, you may live in an urban area. Whether you live in a city, a suburb, or rural area, there are lots of ways to get connected and tune in to nature.

Urban Nature

In many Pagan circles, the wilderness is held up as a source of magical power and the ideal setting for Pagans to live and practice. Cities are portrayed as evil symbols of patriarchy and

58

industrialization, devoid of spirit. While many Pagans travel outside of the cities to commune with nature, hold rituals, and attend gatherings, it isn't necessary to go that far. The sacred is all around. We need only to be aware of it, which may be as easy as shifting our perspective.

Let our eyes become new again, and see for the first time that nature is everywhere. Nature is irrepressible. Like the dandelion growing up between the cracks of the sidewalk, or the wildflowers sprouting at the base of the signpost, natural energy is persistent, vibrant, and contagious.

Green Spaces

Most North American cities now incorporate the "green city" concept into their urban planning. Parks, plazas, and green spaces all contribute to a healthier city.

In San Diego, the Partners for Livable Spaces recently held a "Greening the City: Love It or Leaf It Conference." The conference focused on the critical need to plan for sustainable development and promote a better understanding of the economic, environmental, and psychological benefits of parks, gardens, greenbelts, trails, and inspired green urban spaces. Most neighborhoods have parks and playgrounds, and school yards incorporate living, breathing green spaces. There are also green spaces attached to universities, churches, and cemeteries, which are usually quiet and safe.

Urban Agriculture

Community gardens are an exciting way to reconnect with the Earth. Land that is owned by the city, utility companies, or even abandoned land can be used for community gardens, where measured plots are rented or assigned to individuals. Individuals plant and tend to their own garden plots.

Studies by social researchers reveal that there are links between access to gardens, the building of community bonds, and an overall improvement in social and mental health.

Through community gardens, people have opportunities for education, awareness, and action. They build friendships, trade produce and stories. And as they enjoy increased access to natural spaces, community gardeners come to appreciate the genuine beauty of green space and the connection between gardening, ecology, and community building.

Community gardens also help to build the fabric of the social economy—initiatives and actions that are organized and controlled locally and are not-for-profit. The social economy gets things done and creates relationships between people, bringing them together to identify and to take cooperative action on local problems. Gardening together creates healthy social bonds.

City-wide Wilderness

Whether you go alone or take a friend or your children with you, the following activities can help you to become aware of natural cycles and the energies that are all around us.

- Keep a journal of urban wildlife sightings. City dwellers often include: chipmunks, squirrels, raccoons, skunks, groundhogs, porcupines, and a huge variety of birds, rodents, and insects.

- Take a "herb walk." Look for mint, catnip, dandelion, chamomile, sweet grass, comfrey, yarrow, lemon balm, sumach, and tansy. If picking herbs for your own use is allowed, make tinctures, ointments, soaps, and balm from the herbs you've gathered.

- Savor the sights and scents of each season. Smell mud. Look up to see sap drip from a broken branch, and leaf buds swelling riotous and fertile. Look for the tender heads of crocus and snowdrops that push up on the south side of buildings.

- Learn about trees. Notice which species are common to your area, where they like to grow, and try to figure out how old they are.

- Learn the location of publicly owned fruit trees and bushes, and make a note to return there during their fruiting season. Common trees include apple, crab apple, elderberry, raspberry, blackberry, gooseberry, currents, and pears.

- Preserve jellies, jams, and chutneys so that you can always have a little taste of summer even in the dead of winter.

- Listen to the rustle of autumn leaves and the enchanted musical buzz of wasps hovering around ripened fruits.

- Invite a friend or family member out with you one day and share some of your sacred spaces with them.

- Watch the snow fall, and walk on the fresh snow in streets. Feel the winter air sear your lungs awake with each inhalation.

- Gather small mementos of your journeys, imbued with the energy and enjoyment of your learning. Place them on your altar as a reminder of nature's importance and continual presence.

Stay Safe in Nature

While we hold an image of nature being nurturing and good, there are dangers in nature that are not to be ignored. When you venture outdoors, always plan for safety. Whether you trek into the wilderness of bush and mountains, or into the wilderness of the urban jungle, make plans for your own safety, and always plan ahead.

If you are heading out on your own, let a friend know about your travel plans and when you will return. That way, if you go missing, someone will know. If you are venturing into a new area, prepare ahead of time by consulting a map and knowing your route. And don't be shy: ask for directions. It is a great way to meet locals. Be prepared for the unexpected, and carry basic necessities with you: change for a pay phone, or a cell phone to call for help if needed, a small snack and a bottle of water to provide for the body, any medication you regularly take, identification, enough money to get some-where else, and a little card that says whom to call in case of an emergency.

And, when you are prepared, get outside. Let nature inspire and enliven you, ground and balance you. Absorb the real magic of nature.

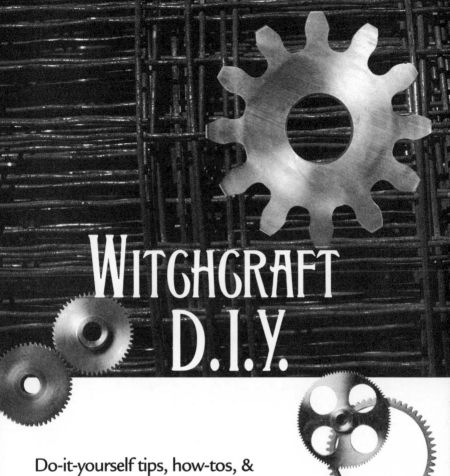

WITCHCRAFT
D.I.Y.

Do-it-yourself tips, how-tos, &
empowering instructions for
the extremely Witch-minded

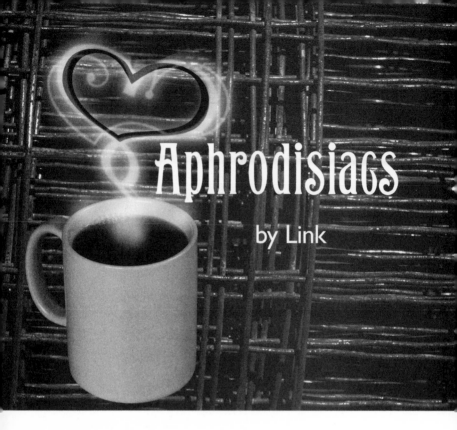

Aphrodisiacs

by Link

For thousands of years, people have handed down home remedies for a variety of purposes, including aphrodisiacs. While some aphrodisiacs reportedly have real affects, they are far from the fabled Love Potion. Aphrodisiacs commonly fall into two categories; they're either an herb or a food. But there are others.

Herbal Aphrodisiacs

Aphrodisiac herbs are taken as teas or dietary supplements, which cause changes in the body or the mood to enhance lovemaking. Some have medicinal effects, like increasing blood flow to the reproductive areas. But as with any herbal mix, we should remember that the medicinal property is only one aspect. Herbs are the dried remains of a plant that was once a living, breathing being. Plants are like people; they're a complex mix of body, mind, and soul. They radiate unique energies. So, when  you think of an herb, try to think of its whole being, not just its leafy green body. Talk to your herb. Connect with its spirit. And let it connect with you.

Some herbs that are considered aphrodisiacs, like ginseng, garlic, and guarana, also offer numerous other benefits. Perhaps these multi-purpose "friends" remind us that some plants are just naturally rich in nature's energies. Like little batteries, general-purpose herbs store magical energy that we can direct according to our needs. Whenever you devote the time and effort, the planning and expense, the intent and desire to brew a magical cup of tea to accomplish a specific goal, you are directing the energies within the tea's ingredients toward that goal. Remember that if you chose it, anything can be an aphrodisiac.

First Comes Food, Then Comes Love

As foods, aphrodisiacs have all the characteristics we discussed for herbs, but also have a nutritional aspect. We all learned that carrots are good for your eyes, and calcium is good for your teeth and bones. But what nutrients are important for healthy sex organs?

Nutrition, an important pre-cursor to any aphrodisiac, is the perfect example of Maslow's hierarchy (the hierarchy of human needs, beginning with basic physical needs and progressing toward self-actualization). We are reminded that we often need to get the basics in order before we can progress to more complex states. General health is important to good sex. Who wants to make love when we have the flu? But don't limit health to physical health. Often we need the peace of mind, body, and spirit in order to be our best. High stress and a general inability to cope with life's mundane demands can make it hard to feel sexy.

Foods are perhaps the most multi-faceted aphrodisiacs available. Chewy. Salty. Sweet. Sticky. Moist. Warm. Cool. Foods can be very sexy.

Sensory Aphrodisiacs

Sometimes what you hear can all help set the mood, whether it's music, conversation topics, or even those lovely little purring noises people make when they are happy. What we see can be very stimulating, too. When we share a form of erotica, or when we become a form of erotica for our partner through sexy clothing and provocative movements, we're setting a mood.

Who could doubt the power perfumes and incense have to kindle passion's flames? And don't forget touch. *Touch*—even the sound of the word is sexy. Gentle massage, affection—*cariño*. To add to the effect, try wearing something made of materials that enhance touch, something satiny and soft.

And Then There's Magic!

Many aphrodisiacs are not instant fixes. They are part of a process that needs to be repeated over the course of weeks or months to take effect. It is easy to understand the medicinal and nutritional reasons for the repetition, but repetition also has magical significance. Repeating a magical act over and over gives it more power, like the way a dancer improves by practicing a specific move many times. Practice makes perfect. Repetition builds a reservoir of power that makes that act even more potent (like adding reps to your exercise workout helps tone muscles). Rather than just one cup of tea, take one cup of tea each day for a week, or perhaps an entire lunar cycle. It's no accident that the word "spell" is used for both a magical act and a period of time.

Unlike home remedies we take just for ourselves, an aphrodisiac is something that involves a partner. Its chemistry is affected by the chemistry shared between the couple. What works with one partner might not with another. Experiment to see what aphrodisiac best fits you and your loved one. Make it a shared experience. Grind the herbs together, mixing in a bit of your own essence as you stir the mortar and pestle in circular motions. Share the cup as you drink, perhaps by lifting the cup to your partners lips, or feeding them sensuously.

Remember that our food and drink becomes a part of us. They race through our bloodstream and join with our bodies, becoming a part of our muscles, tissue, hair, and nails. So when you pick up a juicy morsel of food and feed it to your partner in an attempt to create romance, you are magically charging an item that your partner will carry with them for a long, long time.

The Power of Ritual

by Raven Digitalis

Every Witch is a little different. Some are raised in family systems, some join traditions with acute methods of training, some prefer solitary study, and others take an eclectic approach and integrate elements from many spiritual paths. Regardless of what type of Witch or Wiccan one is, the fact remains true that we all need some form of discipline. For those who have studied and practiced the Old Ways for many years, personal discipline is more appealing in terms of perceived legitimacy. For people new to the path—especially those not belonging to a strict Craft tradition—personal discipline is easily questioned. While numerous practitioners may speak highly of the benefits of "crackin' down," newbies are a bit more wary, which is understandable due to a lack of hands-on experience.

High spiritual acts (like fasts, tonsures, and vows) are immensely rewarding if properly approached. But these sorts of things are both foreign and intimidating to a person just beginning to delve into the Arts. Even the constant, strict sabbat and esbat observations can seem a bit much to a person unaware of the importance of strengthening these natural attunements.

The amount of personal responsibility inherent in the Craft is immense. If one follows Wicca, for example, in an eclectic fashion, the only hard-and-fast guidelines are given in the Wiccan Rede (as well as the Charge of the Goddess and the Witches' Rune, for many practitioners). This, of course, leaves the rest up to us. Our thoughts, daily choices, and methods of interaction are all part of how we walk our path, and properly living the Craft demands that these things be in alignment to our lifestyles as Pagans. Choosing some level of personal discipline is one way in which we align ourselves to the greater cycles of existence, and to a chosen spiritual path.

Daily Devotion

A form of discipline that both experienced practitioners and newcomers can gain a lot from is daily devotion. The most common form of daily devotion is morning ritual.

Though most morning rituals are to greet the start of the day, the more nocturnally minded may choose to do "morning" rituals at 7:00 in the evening! Still, it can be called a "morning ritual" because it's that person's start to the day.

As we awaken, our consciousness is drawn from the dream-scape to the physical. Returning from an ethereal state of being to a solid in-the-present awareness can be a jolting experience. Of course, stimulants like coffee and Yerba Maté can aid us in becoming more aware of our waking state, but at the time of day before these substances are consumed, the time before any food is eaten and before E-mail is checked, is the ideal "between the planes" state of being in which to practice daily devotions.

Some high magick traditions require students to practice some form of daily ritual for a period of a year and a day, or more. For systems that work heavily with Qabalistic magick, this daily ritual is often the Lesser Banishing Ritual of the pentagram, a powerful ceremony in which the practitioner attunes to a direct force of energy that strengthens a rampart of protection about the individual.

A connection to any vibration can be strengthened with a daily devotion.

When a particular ritual is practiced constantly like this, the mechanisms for evoking and invoking the energies become quite natural to the magician. Over time, the practitioner begins to develop a psychic bond with the energies raised and is able to bring these forces forth without necessarily going through all the motions. This, of course, also strengthens psychic ability and makes the working of magick a much smoother process.

On a similar note, many Buddhist schools require the practitioner to engage in meditation for several hours every morning. This makes the person more aware of their physical body existing in the present moment, and draws attention to one's mental processes. Practicing strict and repetitive meditation also helps create a constant meditative state of being in the practitioner.

The above are extreme examples of the potential in performing daily devotions as ritualistic alignments. Though the effects of these sorts of daily devotionals are immense, it's possible to have at least some sort of effect when such precise rituals are not practiced each day. If a person has been studying and practicing

an occult system for some years, their capacity for performing strong, rigid daily rituals is greater. For someone newer to the Arts, a lesser form of direct alignment is more feasible.

Daily devotionals can be tailored to you based on your own experience and needs. What works best for one person may not work for another. If you have enough dedication to practice a morning ritual, be assured that there is plenty of leeway for personal alteration. For example, if you

Aligning to the four elements will provide protection, balance, and spiritual connection . . .

have a particular patron deity, align with that deity every morning to gain a greater connection. If you've had transformational experiences through chanting, singing, or vocal intonation, doing so first thing in the morning may be of great benefit. If a person is gifted at aligning bodily energies, it would be ideal to start the day with a chakra- and aura-cleansing meditation.

Aligning With Energy

The connection to any vibration can be strengthened with a daily devotion. As aforementioned, deities that are attuned to in the morning carry their influence throughout the day. Deities are archetypical vibrational *egregores* (energetic thought forms that can be accessed by simply calling their presence forth, a process of partial invocation). If a person isn't attuned to one particular deity, or just wishes to focus on more terrestrial aspects, the elements earth, air, fire, and water can be attuned to for an energetic boost throughout the day.

One method of connecting with the elements is to call them forth as you would in any other solitary ritual. Instead of inviting their presence for a particular rite, communicate with them on a more personal level. Discover which properties of each element would most benefit you through your day. If you need mental focus, ask the spirits of air to bestow this upon you. If you could use an extra bit of courage in the day's tasks, fire can help instill this strength within.

Aligning to the four elements will provide protection, balance, and spiritual connection; but if you find yourself at a turning point in life, choosing one element to work with may be best. When a single element is worked with, its energy is directly tapped and is not diffused by the properties of the other three. For example, taking seven days (one for each planet) to do an elemental devotion to water can provide emotional healing and empathic blossoming.

At the same time, working with an isolated element for an extended period of time can prove unbalancing. Continuing the above example, a person working constantly with water and no other elements can become emotionally overwhelmed and disconnected to the more stagnant aspects of existence. No magick is beneficial in excess; it's the balance we seek as Witches.

Personalize Your Rituals

There are many variables to work with when forming personalized daily rituals. Ancient Hermetic magicians recognized that each day has a particular ruling planet. In antiquity, only seven planets were known. Their rulerships are as follows:

Sunday: Sun
Monday: Moon
Tuesday: Mars
Wednesday: Mercury
Thursday: Jupiter
Friday: Venus
Saturday: Saturn

By researching the metaphysical properties of one planet each day, you can honor and align to it in daily ritual. Depending on the type of magick you work, creating magickal squares and planetary sigils are ideal in a planetary observation. If you feel drawn to certain deities that rule these planets, working with one each morning would be an invigorating experience.

I feel it is beneficial to practice a planetary attunement of some sort each day of the week for a duration of seven weeks. Not only does this strengthen my connection to the planets through the power of seven, but it serves as good training for remembering planetary properties that are essential to the Witches' craft.

If you choose to align with the planetary vibration of seven for a week, I recommend purchasing a white seven-knob candle, which are available from most Pagan supply stores and mail-order retailers. These candles, which look like naughty toys, are tapers with seven sections of wax, each of which is designed to burn in one session on a single day for a "reinforcement" or "snowball effect" spell. Each knob can be inscribed with the day's astrological symbol (and dressed with oil if you'd like), and it generally takes between one and two hours to fully burn. If a seven-knob candle is unavailable, you may instead take a regular white taper candle and stick seven evenly spaced pins or needles in it. When a needle falls, the section is totally burned. Needle-candle spells have a history in witchcraft and can be used for a variety of purposes including daily rituals.

Continuing the astrological influence, you may want to consider the Moon's aspect when deciding how to structure a morning ritual. If she is waning, it would be a good time to practice a banishing ritual of some sort upon waking. If

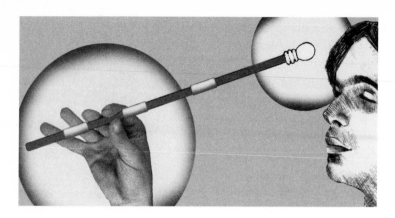

she is waxing, an invocation of a particular energy you wish to cultivate would be appropriate. The sign the Sun is in also has influence, as do the signs other planets are in (and their retrogrades), though in a broader sense.

Morning rituals can be structured very similarly to a spell. In a sense, daily devotionals are in fact miniature spells in that the magician has a goal in mind, whether that be for a particular, acute cause, or simply for spiritual communion.

The duration of time that each person practices a daily devotional ceremony is an entirely personal choice. If a daily devotion is fairly simple, yet meaningful, such as lighting a candle and some incense in the name of a particular energy, the duration of time will be much shorter than performing an all-out morning ritual with elemental calls and hours of meditation. It's up to us to decide what works best for us individually, and to objectively look at what we spiritually need in our lives, even if manifestation of such things (by way of lengthy morning rituals) means waking up an hour earlier than usual!

Another dynamic to consider is the "inside or outside" question. Most Witches prefer to perform rituals outdoors in nature, which would also be extremely beneficial for invoking the morning's solar energy. Outdoor rituals also allow direct elemental influence to occur: the wind blows, the soil supports, the Sun reigns, and water flows, surrounding the practitioner with direct, natural elemental influence. However, if you live in a busy urban area, or are surrounded by less-than-accepting neighbors, practicing a brief ritual outside may invoke more anxiety than balance. Not to mention, many Witches prefer skyclad—"fresh out of the bath"—morning rituals, something that might not go over so well with conservative neighbors who would rather call the cops than the elements!

Because morning rituals are generally less formally structured than spells and other rites, listening to musick (as I spell the word) during the process can be a fun addition to the morning routine. Again, much emphasis on personal preference is placed here. If you prefer mellow, soothing musick (like New Age, Celtic, jazz, ambient, or classical) at the beginning of the day, it can easily be incorporated to add to the ritualistic flow of daily prayer. If you prefer more upbeat musick (like progressive electronic, worldbeat, synthpop, or oldies), an ecstatic dance

Daily devotionals keep us connected to the path we walk, reminding us that magick and spirituality are a part of our every waking (and sleeping) moment . . .

can be incorporated with daily prayer to get the blood flowing, muscles moving, and body grooving. Devotional dances can be performed for a deity or elemental presence; just weave the energy throughout and be creative!

Many people practice yoga, stretching, and other exercises upon awakening. This can also be incorporated in the daily routine to invigorate the body and connect the Self to waking life. The word yoga itself means "unity" or "oneness," in other words, connecting to Spirit. There are various schools of yoga, each emphasizing different aspects of the practice, though none have forgotten yoga's purpose as a spiritual vehicle.

Solitary rituals of any kind—even taking a walk in nature—are so worthwhile because within them it's "only you and Spirit." Solitary workings give the practitioner direct communion with spiritual forces and allow the ego to dissolve more than it would in a public Circle. Because of the power in solitary rituals, the energy can be used to alter the Self and others. If you decide to practice daily devotions as a ritualistic routine, the patterning of such activities will make them that much more natural. When this feeling has been achieved, the energy raised in daily devotions can be redirected from yourself to others, and even the world.

Heal Self First

If we all worked energetically on ourselves first, and then this planet and other people second, the Earth's vibrations would be better able to transcend. Magick follows intention, and visualization is a powerful magickal tool to send it along. Just by envisioning the energy of the world healing and its people becoming wiser, another piece of intention magick is added to the collective consciousness.

While creating your morning rituals, feel free to take the ideas I've mentioned and expand on them, alter them, twist them, and discover what works best for you. Daily devotionals keep us constantly connected to the path we walk, reminding us that magick and spirituality are a part of our every waking (and sleeping) moment, not just during to ritual. By weaving energy and aligning to Deity in small yet consistent intervals, the connection between the human realm and the divine realm becomes more closely interwoven in the collective unconscious. Daily devotions allow us to bloom as the Pagan spiritual conduits we seek to be, and they encourage greater spiritual expansion and self-awareness.

Magical Hemp

by Aar Tiana

Because hemp's plant origins are the same as the illegal drug marijuana, this article will only present working magically with this plant in its imported legal forms, two of which are hemp fiber to make yarn, twine, or fabric, and the nutrient-rich hemp seed oil.

The term "hemp" is also used for different plants, mostly to describe other plant-based clothing fibers (whereas cannabis, meaning "two dogs," was known as the "true hemp"). However, a very different example is Barbarian's hemp (*Sesamum indicum*), which is commonly known as sesame, and in Chinese as *hei zhi ma*. Another example, Indian hemp (*Apocynum cannabinum*), is a poisonous member of the dogbane family that grows mostly in eastern Kansas, and incidentally is an ingredient in some old recipes for Witches' flying ointments. Because of Indian hemp's poisonous tendencies, it is not recommended here. In any case, none of these would be the same plants, and therefore are not considered as any basis for this article.

Properties of Hemp

Latin/Scientific Name:	*Cannabis Sativa*
Common Name(s):	Hemp, industrial hemp, bhang, chanvre, chronic, gallowgrass, ganeb, ganja, grass, hanf, kif, marijuana, neckweed, tekrouri, weed
Legal Forms Explored Here:	Hemp fiber (i.e., yarn, twine, or fabric), and hemp seed oil
Planetary Rulerships:	Saturn, Venus, Jupiter, Neptune
Zodiacal Signs:	Capricorn, Gemini
Constellations:	"Two Dog Stars" of Orion, Canis Major (containing Sirius) and Canis Minor (containing Procyon)
Numerology:	2, 5, 6, 7
Elements:	Earth, water
Holiday Associations:	Litha/Midsummer/Vestalia, Ostara
Direction:	East
Time of Day:	Sunrise

Gods:	Asar/Osiris, Pan, Dionysus/ Bacchus, Priapus, Shiva, Fimbul/Fimbulltyr, Vaithgantas Rupintojelis/Vaizgamtas
Goddesses:	Aset/Isis, Bast/Bastet, Vesta/ Hestia, Venus, Freyja, Indra, Mati-Syra-Zemlya, Amaterasu, Hani-Yasu-No-Kami
Magical Uses:	Hemp has all the qualities of quartz crystal, including magnification or amplification of any magical work, manifestation, "programming" with positive energy, removal of negative energy, healing, love, protection, psychic vision, peace, meditation, beauty, harmnone binding—the possibilities are endless!

History and Lore

On a more mundane level, industrial hemp is very ancient and has been used in many areas of the world as fiber for clothing, and later paper, since approximately 8000 BCE, quite possibly due to its amazing resistance to pests, including mold, weeds, and insects, as well as its weather and climate tolerance, fast growth, and renewing quality. It is also used extensively as food. This history is immense and lush, but we will focus here on hemp's magical uses.

Ancient Japanese Shinto priests used a *gohei* (a short stick with undyed hemp fibers), in purification rites to drive away evil, and hemp was also used to bind marriages and to create happiness. Korean men wore hemp pants, called *paji ma*, for virility and power. In Slavic tradition, in the ancient Don Region, hemp oil was sacrificed to the goddess Mati-Syra-Zemlya, meaning

"moist Mother Earth" or "Mother of the wet Earth" for a good harvest. In northern Europe on Ostara (around March 21), a maiden would honor Freyja by making a hemp wreath, which she tossed onto the doorknob of the house where the man lived whom she wished to attract. A legend from India says hemp came from the heavens via drops of their version of ambrosia that spilled and became hemp plants, and, in turn, were made into a beverage to honor Indra. The African Dogon tribe used hemp in their worship of the constellations, the "Two Dog Stars" of Orion, which are Canis Major (containing the most notable star Sirius) and Canis Minor (containing the most notable star Procyon), due to their legend of a fish-head god who brought them hemp.

Add hemp to your purification blends to get rid of negativity, or even in protection blends, and don't forget to add some to Midsummer's ritual incense.

Interestingly, this God said he came from what today is known as Sirius B (the white dwarf star), discovered by scientists hundreds of years later. Even more interesting is the relationship between Sirius A (the star we see) and Sirius B, in that their paths create an intertwining similar in proportion with the intertwining of DNA, the fabric of the universe. In modern-day Pagan, Wiccan, and witchcraft books, hemp is mentioned as an ingredient in many old incense recipes and resonates with Midsummer, which falls approximately June 21 in the Northern Hemisphere.

Practical Uses for Hemp

Hemp possesses a magical energy very similar to clear quartz crystal. This property comes from the shape of the fiber. If a portion of hemp fiber is "sliced" like a loaf of bread and placed under a microscope, you'd see a hexagon shape, as opposed to a circular shape that is common to most fibers. However, since hemp is more flexible in its fiber form, and more liquid in its seed oil form, it is much more versatile! Use hemp seed oil alone or blended with any of your other ritual, anointing, or magical oils. I have noticed that hemp seed oil is an excellent addition to money oil, or any blend in which the fastest, yet safest, route to manifestation is desired. Remember that hemp magnifies and manifests your magic—use accordingly.

Manifest With Hemp
Use some hemp fibers in your magical incense blends to magnify or manifest (i.e. "weave" into existence) your desires faster and to increase psychic visions.

Use in Protection and Binding Rituals
Add hemp to your purification blends to get rid of negativity, or even in protection blends, and don't forget to add some to Midsummer's ritual incense. Because hemp fibers are known to be strong, you can use the yarn or twine itself in harm-none binding rituals, such as handfastings. You can wrap and charge candles (either deosil or widdershins, depending on your magic), ritual tools like your athame handle, and even your wand. For those of you who smudge with whole herbs, increase your magic by using hemp twine or yarn to wrap your herbal "wands" before burning.

Cord Magic

Knotwork (cord magic) is something else that hemp lends itself well to, particularly if you use hemp twine (and hemp takes to natural dyes well). Because knotwork is a very powerful manifestation tool, you can also use techniques like macramé, tatting, and crochet instead of a rope with knots; then you have something useful and magical at the same time! Also, if you can find hemp fabric, it allows its own type of versatility, although it is usually somewhat expensive. Experiment away!

My Experiences Using Hemp in Magic

Since I crochet with hemp often, I am very familiar with the "feel" of an item that is magically charged by me as I create it. Healing energy pours out of my hands while I handle the yarn, which goes along with my mental intentions for love, light, and healing to the recipient, even if I don't know who that person is. And hemp really makes it "stick"—no doubt due to its quartz crystal/Saturn qualities. For example, if on a waning Moon Friday (for beauty—Venus) I decide to crochet a small hemp facial scrubbie, not only is this practical for washing my face, but while making it, I can infuse my magical intentions to remove psychic and physical impurities as well as allowing my true beauty to surface. (Hemp is also mold-resistant.) Please keep in mind that hemp's "stickiness" can be a disadvantage when trying to clear and reprogram; therefore, take extra time and care.

Make Your Own Crocheted Hemp Scrubbie

Here is a beginning crochet pattern to make a crocheted hemp scrubbie. First, obtain a small amount of hemp yarn, scissors, and a size-H crochet hook.

To begin, chain 10.

Row 1: Half double crochet in the 2nd chain from hook, and each chain across (9 half double crochets).

Rows 2–8: Chain 1, turn, 1 half double crochet in each half double crochet across.

Finishing: Chain 14, join with slip stitch in same corner to form a loop to hang it for drying, chain 1, turn, 14 single crochets inside of the loop, slip stitch to corner again, fasten off, weave in ends, and you are ready to use it for your intended purpose!

This scrubbie pattern is easily converted to a washcloth. Begin with chain 22 (or a number near there that means something to you, plus 1 for turning), crochet straight rows to form a square, and make the hanging loop by stitching 20, rather than 14 stitches. Finish accordingly. These washcloths are superb for the kitchen or the bath.

You may notice while crocheting hemp yarn that excess yarn fuzz and twigs either fall off or need to be pulled off. Don't throw these fibers away, use them magically instead. They work very well for incense and herbal blends created with intention.

Crocheted Sun

I have also crocheted a hemp yarn "sun" in ritual to represent the Sun God that gets burned in the ritual fire. Even if you don't crochet, hemp is a great fiber for this. Just wrap it around cardboard a few times, make a few well-placed knots, cut the strings, and you have a hemp version of a corn dolly! (You can use numerology here if you wish—for instance, 120 times so it keeps the numerological value of 12.)

If you wish to crochet a sun, obtain a small amount of hemp yarn, scissors, and a crochet hook (size-J is great, but use whatever size you feel comfortable with).

To begin, chain 4.

Round 1: Make 11 double crochets in the 4th chain from the hook (in other words, the first chain stitch you made). Join with a slip stitch to the 3rd or the top chain stitch. You will have 12 "spokes" to work with, which resonates with the solar calendar year.

Round 2: Chain 4, 1 double crochet in the next double crochet (from Round 1), then [chain 1, 1 double crochet in the next double crochet] 11 times, chain 1, and slip stitch to the 3rd chain in the beginning of Round 2. End off, you are done!

Approximately 90 percent of the crocheting I do is creating headwear for others, whether I use hemp or not. When I crochet a piece for someone, I "tune in" on them and their spiritual needs, and due to this, I vary my intentions to bring the person's upper chakras into alignment, to open their spiritual growth, and to allow for healing in all forms—especially physical healing, if they underwent chemotherapy and likely wear hats to cover their heads while they regrow hair. I have done this so much that it automatically happens now!

Crocheting hemp can be another way for your magic wishes and desires to be carried to spirit (rather than writing on paper.) In fact, I attended a Lakota sweat lodge ritual called an *inipi* (meaning to be cleansed and reborn from the Earth), and we made prayer bundles to throw into the ritual fire. Prayer bundles are simply pinches of tobacco wrapped in cotton cloth. With permission from the spirits, I crocheted some hemp into a sun shape with intention, put that with my tobacco, wrapped my prayer bundle with more hemp, and threw it in the fire for the smoke to carry my prayers for healing the land to the spirits. I believe Spirit heard and definitely answered! Within the month, the area where the inipi was held burned to the ground during the record-breaking San Diego fires! This is not "exactly" what I had asked for, and I am positive that others had also placed intentions for healing the land; however, even with a disruption as major as that, Spirit had apparently seen it to be the fastest way to heal the land, as well as the people. Such an outpouring of love happened after that, and love is what truly heals! And the plant life is returning in full-force now, so the land is healing, as well as the people of the land!

. . . please be very careful what you wish for—hemp delivers!

This article is intended to inspire you to integrate and harness the very versatile, and powerful, magical energy of hemp, and thereby help you to expand your magical practice. However, please be very careful what you wish for—hemp delivers!

For Further Study

Cunningham's Encyclopedia of Magical Herbs, by Scott Cunningham. Llewellyn Worldwide, 1984.

The Complete Book of Incense, Oils and Brews, by Scott Cunningham. Llewellyn Worldwide, 1989.

Hemp! For Textile Artists, by Cheryl Kolander. Mama D.O.C. Inc., 1995.

Internet Resources

"How to Crochet" at http://www.crochet.com/lessons/lesson.html.

"Crochet Pattern Central" at http://www.crochetpatterncentral.com.

"The Emperor Wears No Clothes" at http://www.jackherer.com/chapters.html.

Building Shadows
by Skyewolf

A Witch's Book of Shadows: that mysterious grimoire that holds all the information a Witch will ever need, a volume of all the spells ever written, the magic of the ages bound together with paper and ink hidden away for centuries and passed from mother to daughter through secret ritual . . .

Piffle! It is not some ancient arcane book that you will come across covered with dust and buried in the back room of your local antique store, and if you did I'd steer clear. Not knowing the previous owner or general energy of any magical item is bad news unless you've got some good background in cleansing. Even then, in my opinion, it's always better to start fresh. Anything that comes from your own hand will always have your own special energies attached to it and it will always be uniquely yours.

Yes, a Witch's Book of Shadows contains spells and information intended to be used for your reference, but it should grow and evolve with you. When you begin, and possibly for some time after, your Book of Shadows will be nearly empty. When and what you fill it with is, by and large, up to you. What follows is my own personal method of creation when it comes to my Book of Shadows; you may use it as a place to begin, but remember that "personal" is the important word. You should work to tailor your book in ways that make it work best for you.

I like to start off my Book of Shadows with a blessing of protection for the book as well as its contents. The nature of the spell or blessing is left up to you. My protections are mainly for the purpose of prying eyes and curious fingers. Enough to give it a general aura of "Do Not Touch." You don't want everyone picking it up and leafing through it, even if you are out of the broom closet and don't care who knows it. Remember that objects pick up energy from the people who handle them and the last thing you want is random deposits of negativity left by someone who just happened to be having a bad day.

If you are so inclined you can follow your blessing with the Wiccan Rede or any other devotion you feel is appropriate. Mine contains the Charge of the Goddess, as well as my more personal devotion to my own goddess. After that, I keep a stack of loose-leaf notebook paper nearby for note taking, as well as a pad of graph paper for keeping track of tarot readings.

Traditionally, a Book of Shadows was no more than a Witch's spell book, and, while contemporary examples do contain spells, they can also become a handy reference volume, housing your astrological charts, color correspondences, herbal lore, and crystal reference. A journal of your spell work is also useful to keep in your Book of Shadows. List your results, the weather, Moon phase, spell reference, and accessories, as well as your personal thoughts and feelings while performing the spell. This can be accessed later, depending on whether or not the spell worked to discover why.

Keep things of interest to you in your Book of Shadows, articles and bits of information, quotes and things that are pertinent to your magical life. Your Book of Shadows should be another of your tools of the Craft. Something you will be able to use in your magical workings. When you plan your Book of Shadows think about what you want to use it for. It will be a process of evolution.

When I began, all I thought about putting in by Book of Shadows was spells. Now I realize that it can be a reference book to use, not just a place to store things and collect dust.

When you think about building your Book of Shadows, choose something large enough so that you will be able to read what you have written. I remember that I began with this tiny hardbound journal from my local bookstore, and I wrote in green ink. It was horrible to read by candlelight! I have since switched to a 2½-inch, three-ring binder that I covered with green cloth and decorated to my liking. Anything I keep in it is printed on the computer in an extra-large type to be easily readable. Using a three-ring binder makes it easy to move things around, add or take away things that need to be changed.

I have given you a few hints and tips, but there is no hard and fast rule about how to make a Book of Shadows. Below is a small list of things I believe should be included in your Book of Shadows but, please remember, this is your book and, in the end, you decide what goes in, what stays out, and what it looks like.

And remember to always be flexible in your views, and don't wait to change something that isn't working or doesn't feel right. You get out what you put in and that goes doubly for your Book of Shadows. With patience, care, and forethought, your Book of Shadows will grow to be your greatest magical asset. You may want to include:

Book Blessing
Magical Correspondence Tables
Oils
Crystals

Incense
Herbs
Colors
Moon phases
Day of the Week
Correspondences
Spell Work Journal
Tarot Journal
Spells
List of Magical
Suppliers
List of Useful
References
Books
Articles

Web Sites
Successes
Spells
Readings
Meditations
Astral Projection

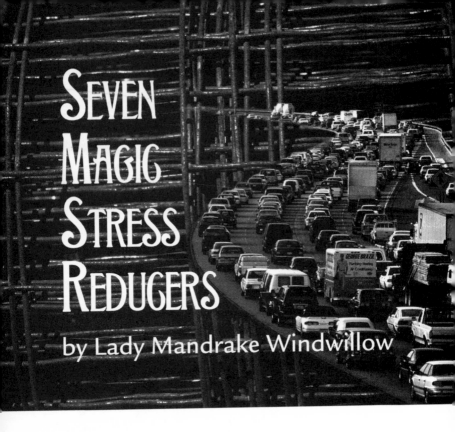

Seven Magic Stress Reducers

by Lady Mandrake Windwillow

Stress caused by our lifestyle and culture plagues us all in one way or another. Stress can cause muscle tension, illness, depression, and high blood pressure, along with promoting use of alcohol, drugs, tobacco, food, and other addictions. We, as magical folk, can use our divinely given talents to help ourselves and those around us reduce the stress in our world. Here are seven simple ways anyone can create a little stress-free magic in their lives.

Meditate

Most Pagan traditions use meditation as part of their daily practices, so it makes sense to incorporate stress reduction into those practices. If you don't practice daily meditation, then a good reason to begin is stress reduction. Daily meditation will also improve  your ability to focus and to raise energy when it's needed for spell working and ritual. Before you begin a daily meditation ritual, take a few minutes to clear your mind of the stresses that could keep you from enjoying your meditation time. Over time, this practice will result in more productive and relaxing meditations.

Take Time

Take back time for yourself. Every person on this planet has the power to take personal time, but few do. This causes stress. Even if you can only steal away five or ten minutes a day, doing so will help you feel more cared for and relaxed.

Walk

Take a walk every day (if possible). Walking is excellent exercise, and it is a great stress reliever. It gets the blood pumping and arms and legs going. If the weather is less than pleasant take a walk around a local mall or museum or take the stairs at your office instead of the elevator. The idea is to get outside and commune with Mother Nature, and if it's blizzard conditions outside, then at least you'll keep your muscles working for when it is nice.

Listen to Music

Listen to music while you are doing mundane activities. Most chain stores now carry CDs and cassettes of relaxing music (usually near the candles) for minimal cost. Play relaxing music or nature sounds that appeal to you. This will take your mind off of the mundane work you are performing and will allow you to relax and let your mind wander. Some employers allow music to be played at a low volume while working. If you have a choice in the music, use music to inspire creativity and productivity without stress and frustration.

Use Aromatherapy

Use scent and aromatherapy in high-stress areas in your home. If you hate doing the dishes and cooking stresses you out, use pleasant-scented dish soap or simmer some relaxing potpourri on the stove (make sure to keep adding water) to let the power of scent relax and invigorate you. There are aromatherapy dish detergents on the market, or you can make your own using scented or essential oils in plain-scented dish detergent. Even at the office you can place a vanilla-scented candle or a bowl of potpourri on your desk (if you cannot burn a candle). If you work as a service person and do not have a desk, wear relaxing oil instead of perfume, and make sure you carry the bottle with you for touch ups during the day.

Take a Relaxing Bath

Use your bathing time to your advantage. Instead of taking a quick shower ten minutes before you have to run out the door, arrange your schedule so you have time for a leisurely bath the night before. Lock the door, light candles, play music, have a bubble bath, and relax. If you prefer showers, use a scented body wash that is pleasing to your senses and let the heat of the water relax all the stress away.

De-stress Your Home

Create a home where stress is not allowed to dwell. Magically charge your home to repel stress as you would any other form of negativity. Do not allow stress to live in the corners or lurk in the shadows. Burn cleansing incenses often and do ritual cleansings when you feel the stress levels building up. By keeping your home a stress-free sanctuary, you have a place to always escape to and feel safe.

These are only a few suggestions on how to use simple commonsense magic to help alleviate the stress that can cause damage if unchecked. You do not need to do all of these for results; try using one and see how it works for you, then add another if you wish. I hope you find the secrets to a stress-free life (and if you do make sure you E-mail me the secret).

Reclaiming the Divine

by Diana Rajchel

I know the exact day my marriage ended—even the time. It was in July of 2001. A drought had crossed southern Minnesota—one so severe that crops were dying and wells were going dry. The day before, I'd sprinkled some rice over a chalk circle and muttered an invocation. This day, the first drops of rain fell from a gloriously overcast sky. At last, water to break the drought. When I returned home from work, I found a box addressed to me and opened it. I was still smiling when my husband walked in the door.

"I have good news and bad news," he said.

I have always preferred to get the worst part over with first. To this day, I still eat my vegetables before any other part of the meal.

"Tell me the bad news," I said.

"I was just laid off from my job."

"So what's the good news?"

"I was offered a job on overnights," he said.

I paused to think about this before I asked, "What about our marriage?"

I said this while holding a miniature scythe. Death came and placed that scythe in my hand. Only a year after that conversation I found myself packing to leave.

A Spiritual Crisis

Initiatory religions, for all their differences, have two things in common: mystery and crisis. Without crisis, the soul has no reason to develop spiritually. Without crisis, the spirit becomes complacent, calmly watching the world as though it's a television show.

Earlier, as a nineteen-year-old first pursuing Wicca, I thought I'd seen a significant crisis in my family's resistance to my adult independence and my few failed relationships. But I was still fundamentally the same safe and unchallenged soul. I was so complacent I didn't realize that I was until a few years later, when all the things I thought I'd struggled for were swept away like sand in a windstorm. And as the dust of my dying life settled around me, I found myself choking on the old safe stuff of my life.

Initiation does more than effect profound changes in a person's outlook.

A series of not-quite coincidences piled up on me at that phase of my life. I performed poorly in my graduate

school program. I fell in love with a man of a different religion and culture than myself. I recognized a long-ignored unhappiness that welled deep within me, and, upon that recognition, I knew how much my life had to change.

Gone were my dreams of a career in journalism. Gone was the stable marriage. Gone were my assumptions about the rightness of my life. Also gone was my sureness of faith. After this major crisis, which left me ill to the point of being crippled, I wasn't sure whether or not the Goddess really had all that much interest in me and my problems.

Initiation does more than effect profound changes in a person's outlook. Destiny itself becomes altered as the thousands of possible realities are shifted into an upward spiral of new possibilities. While in theory I knew all this before parts of my life fell apart, it's impossible to know all until one experiences the extremes—joy so exalted no drug can compare, and sorrow so deep it both cuts and smothers.

In this instance, I set off with initiations boiling in my bloodstream, ready to burst out of me in a ball of personal darkness. The darkness had to happen so I could see light, recognize change, and come to the full realization of how deeply I had changed.

Changing Perspectives

None of these dramatic events happened all at once. I don't think anyone who knows the Goddess really decides not to place any phone calls for a while. Gradual shifts and changes brought the changes so quietly that I did not notice them until they were impossible to ignore. Initially, I thought I was simply burned out on the Wiccan community, and preferred instead to devote my time to "other pursuits."

During this time of "other pursuits," my daily practice tapered off until I couldn't say when there was a Full Moon. This was encouraged by my ex-husband's gentle pressure on me to abandon community work and much of my private practice; he'd always had a strange concern I could become overdependent on magic. We could easily have continued as we were until all the magic I'd worked hard to learn was quietly erased—the candles burnt away, the herbs spoiled and tossed, and my tools tucked into the attic. Then, as cliché as it is, 9/11 happened, and this historical event triggered a series of changes in my life that made me recognize that my very soul was slipping away.

In your Pagan journal you must write toward the life you crave in the future as though it exists in the present.

I was living in a less-than-open-minded prairie town in the Midwest and working for an international student office where the majority of the students I served were Muslims. While 9/11 was not my personal crisis, it marks for me the crises that followed soon afterward. I was already drifting away from my goddess, and it would be a long journey to get back to her.

Two Years Later . . .

I was with my friend Beth in her backyard. Beth had just miscarried a child she desperately wanted, and I literally ran away from work to be with her that day. I had poured out my soul to her and spent an obnoxious amount of my time crying. It was a New Moon, and we invoked Hecate. Hecate proceeded to channel through Beth, chiding her for her grief and fears, and then she started in on me:

"You've forgotten who you are," she said. "And you don't think to ask, who am I?"

Across a huge divide created by me, I felt the Goddess. (This Goddess eventually became a chasm between myself and Beth, who believes wholly in the reality of the Goddess, but worries about the possibility of hell.) My ability to sense the wave I knew as Goddess had dwindled, and I hadn't even noticed until she chose to channel through my uninitiated friend Beth rather than through me.

Making myself soul-willing to enter cooperative service is a longer road than just knowing and having joy in the Goddess.

I renewed my prayer practice after that visit. I also began to try to root through all my blocks and sorrows. I knew the Goddess never leaves her own, but I had left the Goddess and I needed to find my way back.

Returning to the Goddess

Finding my way back to her took swallowing my ego. I had to admit I had come too far—alone, and now I needed help to come back. My prayers were simple: *Let me know you. Let me see you. Let me feel your divinity.*

I also made the decision to return to my community. Even though my private beliefs and politics differ wildly from those of my Pagan neighbors, we are still a city within this city; they are my tribe. I had lied to myself by trying to live in worlds I didn't belong in and trying to form connections with people I just could not form bonds with. Still, I was reluctant to give up many of those relationships because I had so few social connections.

Even though it took a while to find welcome in a local community, I kept at creating new relationships. And I deliberately began to drift from connections that were skeptical (or nearly hostile) about my religious practice. I began to volunteer in activities, and I put myself in a position where I had to speak with people.

Remembering the Divine

Some time after my divorce, I was standing on a street corner in Little Canada, Minnesota, and watching a lunar eclipse with some local members of a Pagan university group. As the Moon faded from view, I performed the final severance ceremony that completed my divorce on a spiritual level. As I glanced up, I saw the head of a lion around the hole of the Moon.

"Hey Mike," I called over my shoulder to the Kemetic priest standing behind me, "Sekhmet wants to talk to you."

The Goddess never left me. None of the gods in any of their forms abandoned me, not really. I had abandoned them in my shame and guilt, but they are ever-present and ready to tap me anytime. Making myself soul-willing to enter cooperative service is a longer road than just knowing and having joy in the Goddess. The Kemetic priest became a hand extended in help to get me back to that path.

Hitch on the Road Back

During all of this, my progress in reconnection was slowed by the development of chronic idiopathic urticaria, which involves a painful skin condition. I was itchy beyond Benadryl, and this sometimes made ritual impossible. I spent at least half my time simply wishing for a cure, wishing for a life where I was not crawling out of my skin. This made old routines difficult at best. I couldn't sit to meditate some days because of hives on my bottom, and other days I couldn't perform standing yoga poses because of hives on my feet.

All of this made my progress, my reconnection, slower and more difficult. It's hard to open to divine love when you're blaming the divine for an improbable, life-hobbling condition.

There were good days, when it appeared I had remission. But the connection I'd built with her over hundreds of rituals, hours of prayer and meditation, and years of reading and study could not be reestablished in a few days. My life had changed fundamentally, and so had I. While I still adhere to the Wiccan path, I am far from the same person who began that journey. I formed new ideas and questions, new doubts, and a belief in new possibilities. I knew that reading what I'd already read and performing rituals with only rote intent would set me farther from the divine, rather than bringing me closer. So I set out to find new ways of thinking about what I thought I already knew.

Her voice came, quietly, like the whisper of far away bells.

Days in the Wilderness

In October of 2003, I isolated myself from everyone and everything except what was necessary to maintain myself. After ten years living as a Wiccan, Samhain season was deeply embedded in my mind, but choosing October as my time of hermitage was not a conscious decision. It was truly an appropriate time, though. This death of my social self gave me time to experience the birthing pangs of my new self and to preserve my dignity in the face of the difficulties I experienced.

My days were simple. I went to work. I returned home. At home, my day began with prayer. I used verses from the www. worldprayer.org Web site. I lit candles and proceeded with breathing exercises and deep meditation. Sometimes all I could manage was to take one hundred deep breaths, and then I'd go to bed. Other days I could continue longer and enjoy a sense of divine ecstasy.

After the divorce, I had very little furniture left, but I decided to keep my surroundings ascetic. I lived as simply as I could.

This alone-time, away from emotional and psychic barrage, gave me time to rebuild my shields and pay attention to

my thought patterns. When I spent time thinking about sacred concepts, I felt better both physically and emotionally. I was not cured by any means, but I was stronger. I felt the slow post-ritual buzz that comes from the injection of genuine emotion into a ritual experience.

Plugging back into that divine energy did not come easily. Cleaning house in my relationships and lifestyle was only the first step, and as with any drastic change, backslides happened. I'd say I'd no longer take phone calls from one person, or answer E-mails from another, only to find myself doing so anyway.

At the end of that October, I was laid off from my job, and I experienced the most unstable period of my life. I'd often forge ahead with my spiritual practice only to set it all aside in the crashing wave of anxiety and illness. I had to rebuild both habit and faith in order to hear the voice of the Goddess.

The Goddess Whispers

Her voice came, quietly, like the whisper of far away bells. My old spiritual caprice returned. I had sudden urges to take a left turn off my usual walking path, or to go out when I'd planned to stay in. I started recognizing weather phenomena and the messages inherent in them again.

No single spell or prayer could reunite me with my divine self or with the divine outer.

The shape of clouds amidst the skyscrapers once again held divinatory meaning. A crow landing in a park was a message delivered.

I returned, slowly, to my belief that the universe has meaning that I could interpret, and that my connection to that universe meant that I too play an important role in its processes and execution.

Still, I sought to hear her more clearly. I went to a Rosen therapist who was patient with me and interested in my Pagan spirituality; this helped with many of my physical and emotional blocks. I also reintroduced a practice of chanting through the seven major chakras every day as a way of clearing myself spiritually and physically.

While no one single act cleared me totally, I returned slowly to a functional lifestyle; and with the awareness of the Goddess' presence, a glimmer of light piercing my gray outlook, I was suddenly on an upward swing again.

At last I ended my hermit-time and returned to the Pagan community, ready to serve. I committed to a local student group, sometimes teaching 101 classes. I picked up my books on Wicca and magic. I became interested again. I started asking questions again. I wanted to know more, hear more, and feel those moments of divine love that I remembered from before my isolation.

No single spell or prayer could reunite me with my divine self or with the divine outer. Just as I began a steady path to realization of the Goddess when I first realized I belonged to her family of faith, I had to climb that path again. This time, my path was rockier because I no longer had the padding of a youthful enthusiasm and bright-eyed naiveté. Instead, I saw where the Goddess belonged in my life, and how she was ever-present as bedrock as I made my way through my life.

There is no magic formula, but the Goddess never leaves you. She will outstretch her arms and let you leave her. It is up to you whether to return.

As Doreen Valiente wrote in *The Charge of the Goddess*:

For behold, I have been with you from the beginning
and I am that which is attained at the end of desire.

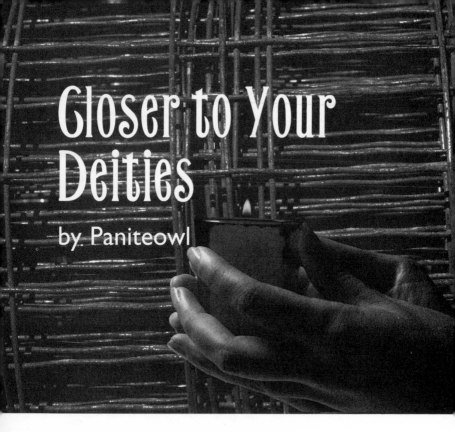

Closer to Your Deities

by Paniteowl

The Pagan community is filled with folks from monotheistic religious backgrounds. The structure of these religions is often so specific that there is little room for the individual to create a personal connection with a deity without following a prescribed format.

Old habits die hard. This can make it difficult for people to find their way along a Pagan pathway, which is often full of spiritual twists, various uncertainties, and vague suppositions. Anyone can totally get confused. It's like taking a road trip with a specific destination in mind when you have no maps or compass by which to chart the journey.

Perhaps the hardest adjustment for those raised with a monotheistic outlook is to embrace the concept of multiple deities. When one has been taught there is but one deity, existing on a plane far above our own, it is very overwhelming to be told that numerous gods and goddesses are everywhere, and quite easy to find if we just look and listen.

Take the First Step

The first thing a confused Pagan should do is ask the deities for help in understanding and awareness. A simple ritual would be to stand under the Full Moon while taking deep cleansing breaths. Open your arms and your heart as you focus your thoughts on truly connecting with everything around you. Feel the air on your skin. Smell the scent of the Earth. Hear the noises of the night. Then ask for help and guidance to walk your spiritual pathway.

The gods and goddesses respond much more quickly to someone who has taken the time to get to know them.

In ancient times, some cultures built elaborate temples to honor their gods and goddesses, yet from the evidence of archeological studies most homes also had altars or small shrines where the deities were included in the everyday patterns of running a household.

This personal connection with deity is something our modern society seems to have lost, yet we can rekindle that spiritual practice. It is quite easy to invite deity into your life by creating sacred spaces in your home. You only need to set aside a bookshelf, a small table, or even a windowsill, and place statuary, pictures representing your deities, and a few candles or sticks of incense on this altar space.

Each day, light a candle or incense, and simply repeat your request for more knowledge and awareness. You'll find that within a short time, the books and articles you are reading and the random conversations you have will begin to reveal glimpses of things you may not have known, or may have overlooked in previous studies.

Keeping a journal is helpful for capturing these moments of awareness. Our lives are so busy that sometimes we forget a thought or a realization almost as fast as we perceive them. It needn't be a fancy leather-bound book; a small note pad or a file you keep on your computer will do.

As we learn about the customs of different cultures, we realize the importance of their spiritual beliefs in activating the deities in their daily life.

Once you start your journal, review your notes and add new perceptions each week. And look for patterns that will lead you to further study of a particular deity or pantheon. Knowing the lore of a deity, as well as the cultural history, will help you to understand and interpret teachings of the gods and goddesses.

The God and Goddess

We are all aware that there is magic and power in a name. We all respond more quickly, and with a more positive attitude, to someone who uses our name to get our attention rather than saying, "Hey, you!" When asking for a deity's patronage, it is a matter of respect to call him or her by name.

The gods and goddesses respond much more quickly to someone who has taken the time to get to know them. Have you ever been to the mall and heard a child cry out, "Mom" or "Dad"? Did you notice how many turn toward that voice? Some will stop, and look to see if the child is in trouble, some

will glance over and keep walking, one or two may even talk to the child to see if they can help.

As we become familiar with more deities, we recognize them on a more personal level. When we call on the God or Goddess, each of us may have a different deity in mind. That's quite all right. Just as we know our parents have formal, legal names, we still call them "Mom" and "Dad."

As we grow we become aware of who our parents are in the greater scheme of things. We learn their names, their jobs, and their personalities. Eventually, we even see them as individuals with feelings, emotions, foibles, and talents. We love them in spite of, and because of, who they are. And if we're very lucky, we come to know them as friends. These are the same stages we go through as we begin our spiritual journey. Our goal is to connect with deity on that very personal basis of familiarity and respect.

Invite the Deity to Your Home

When you invite a guest to your home, there are things you do to make them feel comfortable. You may prepare their favorite meal, place flowers on the table, or light candles to warm the atmosphere. And yes, we all make sure the house is straightened and the bathrooms clean when guests are coming. We shower, and dress appropriately for the occasion, and we show by our actions that our guests are welcomed and cared for. Should we do any less when inviting our deities into our lives?

When celebrating Imbolc, we may invite Bree or Brigit to our ritual. Milk and shepherd's pie may be a good choice for the meal. This is the time of lambing, and the flow of ewe's milk is a significant feature of the holiday.

In the fall, we may invite Diana, the Huntress, so a game pie or venison dinner would be appropriate. During high summer, Bacchus and Dionysus would enjoy the fruit of the vine, so wines would be an important part of the festivities.

At harvest time, we would honor Demeter, and bake breads from the grain she has provided.

As we learn about the customs of different cultures, we realize the importance of their spiritual beliefs in activating the deities in their daily life. We begin to see that our ancestors had a profound personal relationship with their gods and goddesses.

We needn't delve far into the past to see these personal practices. They include such practices as the *mezuzah* on the door of a traditional Jewish home, or the icons from Russia, or the shrines to the Christian Mary found in many homes. We needn't change familiar practices in Pagan practice; we need only to change the focus of those practices to include a wider family of gods and goddesses.

Be Ready for a Few Surprises

Whatever rituals you develop, or habits you create to remind yourself to invite the deities into your life, let me assure you that they all work. The trick is to recognize when the deities truly respond to you! Most of us recognize and remember when some extraordinary thing happened for which we had no plausible explanation other than to say, "Somebody up there likes me." But we often overlook the small blessings we receive, such as finding lost objects, or solving a troublesome and recurrent problem by having a sudden flash of insight.

> I can promise . . . when you seek out the gods and goddesses with sincerity, they do listen and respond.

As we ask for help in connecting with deity, we find that people come into our lives to help us do just that. This is not a random occurrence for one or two people; it is a consistent experience that many of us talk about with others on our paths. After a time, we begin to accept that deity is indeed "meddling" in our lives in many positive ways. Granted, sometimes the input can have chaotic effects, but when we look back we begin to see the patterns and realize there are often signs we overlook as we go about our busy lives. All of us have stories of when we narrowly avoided an accident, or when a gift or change of circumstances happened at a time when we were most in need.

Over time, we realize that this too is a pattern in our lives. We do receive help from our deities every day. Knowing this and accepting their guidance becomes a natural part of our lives, and we truly walk our pathways with confidence. There is one thing I can promise from personal experience: when you seek out the gods and goddesses with sincerity, they do listen and respond.

> **Hecate seemed to be standing at my shoulder with a satisfied smile and a hint of smug satisfaction.**

The Surprise of the Divine

Every once in a while, the gods and goddesses surprise even those of us who work with them every day. I think they like to shake us out of our complacency, just so we never get to a point when we think we know it all. Here's an example I will never forget. I have had a friend for many years whose pathway is different from mine, but we respect each other's practices and have found many similarities in our workings.

She had recently lost her mate of many years and was grieving. I visited to comfort her, and as was usually the case we began talking about how our practices differ. We also talked about our personal experiences with our gods and goddesses and how their personalities influenced our rituals. She mentioned feeling disconnected, and she thought her grief was blocking her awareness of deity.

I offered to do a ritual with her to help her feel at ease, thinking that my focus would help to ground and center her.

As we began the ritual, I called on my patron goddess, Hecate. Now after years of working with Hecate, I am very familiar with her essence. Her personality and attitude may change a bit depending on circumstances, but on the whole there is a consistency in her being. She has warmth, strength, and, yes, even a sense of humor.

As I felt her presence this day, I took a cleansing breath and fell into the familiar pattern of connection—and then I got the surprise of my life. Hecate stepped back and another presence flowed forcefully through me. This was not in an aggressive manner, but it was certainly in a self-assertive way. As she passed she seemed to give me a hug and a nod, which said, "Thanks, Hon, I'll take it from here."

As I parked my car I noticed a bumper sticker on the car in front if me that read "Back off, I'm a goddess."

This was not my first encounter with Kali, but it certainly was the strongest and most pronounced experience I'd ever had with her. I did nothing but stand there with my hands on the shoulders of my friend as Kali swept through her with comfort and assurance.

Meanwhile, Hecate seemed to be standing at my shoulder with a satisfied smile and a hint of smug satisfaction. Kali did something for my friend that day, but that is her story to tell. Hecate then showed me what it was like to be the facilitator, or the assistant, who works behind the scenes.

Defer to the Greater Wisdom

There are times when a priest or priestess must take charge of a situation, and there are times when we must step back and let others experience their own realities. Even with all the studies I had undertaken over the years, it only took that one instant to change my perspective of what it truly meant to

be a priestess of Hecate and Hermes. It started a whole new phase of learning and acceptance.

Another of my favorite stories is pulling into a parking lot at our local Sam's Club. The lot was full but I got a space close to the doors by using my favorite spell: "Goddess Asphalta, fair of face, help me find a parking space!" (This works especially when you're in a hurry.)

As I parked my car I noticed a bumper sticker on the car in front if me that read "Back off, I'm a goddess." There were a few smaller stickers, each one letting me know that the car belonged to someone I'd like to meet, so I sat in my car and waited, knowing in my heart that it wouldn't be long. My teenage grandson, who was with me, rolled his eyes when I told him to just sit for a few minutes to see what would happen.

Within five minutes a woman approached the car carrying some groceries and digging in her purse for her keys. I got out of my car and told her I liked her car. She looked at me, grinned, and said simply, "Do you like the car or the bumper stickers?" We both laughed and then chatted for a bit.

She explained that she was just beginning her journey on the path and had been looking to connect with others. As we talked about local places, events, and people, we realized we did know many of the same people, yet we had never been in the same place at the same time. Then we exchanged phone numbers and talked about where we lived. We both had to laugh out loud when we found out we were neighbors and her property adjoined my land.

We've since become friends and are constantly amazed at the circumstances of our meeting. Her daughter and granddaughter had been to some of my classes years ago, so once again we had "almost" connected with each other—yet as she explains it, she wasn't ready then to really seek out the Pagan community.

In retrospect, however, it's really not all that surprising we met, as she had been seeking her connection with deity. When she was ready to emerge from her solitary practice, circumstances arranged themselves so that we could meet. Once again, I just trust that when the time is right, the deities put us in situations that help us to find solid footing on our paths.

The Trip to the Divine

My journey to deity began almost fifty years ago, and it continues today. I am not the same person I was at the age of fifteen or thirty-five or even fifty.

The people in my life have changed over the years as well. I see old friends and family members as they too move into the crone and sage phases of their lives, and I realize we are all still learning about ourselves and our deities.

As the gods and goddesses give you glimpses of awareness, be assured that these are not figments of your imagination or mere wish fulfillments. Their presence is a very tangible substance in our lives. Each deity may have a particular lesson to teach, but they also bring others to you.

Think of it as having a doctor or counselor who may call in an expert consultant on a specific matter. The old lore tells us of the individual personalities of many gods and goddesses. Their stories also show they worked together for the benefit of our ancestors, to fulfill their needs and guard and challenge them.

Honor that diversity, and rejoice in the fact that we have many deities watching over us. Each has something to show us and teach us. Respect their knowledge and their willingness to share. Enjoy the spiritual realm that surrounds us.

May your journey be as rich and fulfilling as I have found mine, and may it never end as we experience each lifetime with new wonder and amazement. May you find your connection with deity every day of your life.

Almanac Section

spring 2007–spring 2008

spring 2007–spring 2008

spring 2007–spring 2008

spring 2008

The days & the nights, the Moon & the stars, the colors, & all the latest Wiccan/Pagan news—the yearly almanac gives you everything you need to get you through this heady astrological year

With news items written by Dallas Jennifer Cobb

What's Listed in the Almanac
(and How to Use It)

In these listings you will find the date, lunar phase, Moon sign, color, and magical influence for the day. New and Full Moons are shown in bold type.

The Day

Each day is ruled by a planet that possesses specific magical influences:

Monday (Moon): Peace, sleep, healing, compassion, friends, psychic awareness, purification, and fertility.

Tuesday (Mars): Passion, courage, aggression, and protection.

Wednesday (Mercury): The conscious mind, study, travel, divination, and wisdom.

Thursday (Jupiter): Expansion, money, prosperity, and generosity.

Friday (Venus): Love, friendship, reconciliation, and beauty.

Saturday (Saturn): Longevity, exorcism, endings, and houses.

Sunday (Sun): Healing, spirituality, success, strength, and protection.

The Lunar Phase

The lunar phase is important in determining the best times for magic.

The Waxing Moon (from the New Moon to the Full) is the ideal time for magic to draw things toward you.

The Full Moon is the time of greatest power.

The Waning Moon (from the Full Moon to the New) is a time for study, meditation, and little magical work (except magic designed to banish harmful energies).

The Moon's Sign

The Moon continuously moves through the zodiac, from Aries to Pisces. Each sign possesses its own significance:

Aries: Good for initiating things, but lacks staying power. People tend to be argumentative and assertive.

Taurus: Things begun now are lasting, tend to increase in value, and are hard to change. Appreciation for beauty and sensory experience.

Gemini: Time for shortcuts, communication, games, and fun.

Cancer: Stimulates emotional rapport between people. Pinpoints need, supports nurturing. Tends to domestic concerns.

Leo: Draws emphasis to the self, to central ideas or institutions, away from connections with others and emotional needs. People tend to be melodramatic.

Virgo: Favors accomplishment of details. Focuses on health, hygiene, and daily schedules.

Libra: Favors cooperation, social activities, beautification of surroundings, balance, and partnership.

Scorpio: Increases awareness of psychic power. Precipitates psychic crises and ends connections thoroughly. People tend to brood and become secretive.

Sagittarius: Encourages flights of imagination and confidence. This is an adventurous, philosophical, and athletic Moon sign. Favors expansion and growth.

Capricorn: Develops strong structure. Focus on traditions, responsibilities, and obligations. A good time to set boundaries and rules.

Aquarius: Time to break habits and make abrupt change. Personal freedom and individuality is the focus.

Pisces: The focus is on dreaming, nostalgia, intuition, and psychic impressions. A good time for spiritual or philanthropic activities.

Colors For the Day

The colors for the day are based on information from *Personal Alchemy* by Amber Wolfe, and relate to the planet that rules each day. This information can be taken into consideration along with other factors when blending magic into mundane life.

Time Changes

The times and dates of astrological phenomena in this almanac are based on Eastern Standard Time (EST) and Eastern Daylight Time (EDT). If you live outside the Eastern Time Zone, or in a place that does not use Daylight Saving Time, adjust your times:

Central Standard Time: Subtract one hour.

Mountain Standard Time: Subtract two hours.

Pacific Standard Time: Subtract three hours.

Alaska/Hawaii: Subtract five hours.

Areas that have no Daylight Saving Time: Subtract an extra hour from the time given. Daylight Saving Time runs from March 11, 2007–November 4, 2007, and begins again March 9, 2008.

Key to Astrological Signs

Planets		Signs	
☉	Sun	♈	Aries
♃	Jupiter	♉	Taurus
☽	Moon	♊	Gemini
♄	Saturn	♋	Cancer
☿	Mercury	♌	Leo
♅	Uranus	♍	Virgo
♀	Venus	♎	Libra
♆	Neptune	♏	Scorpio
♂	Mars	♐	Sagittarius
♇	Pluto	♑	Capricorn
		♒	Aquarius
		♓	Pisces

Festivals and Holidays

Festivals and holidays are listed throughout the year. When exact dates are unavailable, prevailing data has been used.

2007–2008 Sabbats and Full Moons

March 20, 2007	Ostara (Spring Equinox)
April 2	Seed Moon/Full Moon 1:15 pm
May 1	Beltane
May 2	Hare Moon/Full Moon 6:09 am
May 31	Blue Moon/Full Moon 9:04 pm
June 21	Litha (Summer Solstice)
June 30	Dyad Moon/Full Moon 9:49 am
July 29	Mead Moon/Full Moon 8:48 pm
August 1	Lammas
August 28	Corn Moon/Full Moon 6:35 am
September 23	Mabon (Fall Equinox)
September 26	Harvest Moon/Full Moon 3:45 pm
October 26	Blood Moon/Full Moon 12:51 am
October 31	Samhain
November 24	Snow Moon/Full Moon 9:30 am
December 22	Yule (Winter Solstice)
December 23	Oak Moon/Full Moon 8:15 pm
January 22, 2008	Wolf Moon/Full Moon 8:35 am
February 2	Imbolc
February 20	Storm Moon/Full Moon 10:30 pm
March 20	Ostara (Spring Equinox)
March 21	Chaste Moon/Full Moon 2:40 pm

March 2007

Spring Equinox · March 20

March 20 ♂
Ostara · Spring Equinox
Mabon · Autumnal Equinox
(Southern Hemisphere)
Color: Red

Moon Sign: Aries
Moon Phase: First Quarter

March 21 ☿
Color: White

Moon Sign: Aries
Moon Phase: First Quarter
Moon enters Taurus 1:15 am

March 22 ♃
Color: Green

Moon Sign: Taurus
Moon Phase: First Quarter

March 23 ♀
Color: Pink

Moon Sign: Taurus
Moon Phase: First Quarter
Moon enters Gemini 2:06 am

March 24 ♄
Color: Indigo

Moon Sign: Gemini
Moon Phase: First Quarter

March 25 ☉
Color: Amber

Moon Sign: Gemini
Moon Phase: First Quarter
Moon enters Cancer 5:49 am
Second Quarter: 2:16 pm

☽ **March 26**
Color: Lavender

Moon Sign: Cancer
Moon Phase: Second Quarter

♂ **March 27**
Color: Black

Moon Sign: Cancer
Moon Phase: Second Quarter
Moon enters Leo 1:04 pm

☿ **March 28**
Color: Yellow

Moon Sign: Leo
Moon Phase: Second Quarter

♃ **March 29**
Color: Violet

Moon Sign: Leo
Moon Phase: Second Quarter
Moon enters Virgo 11:27 pm

♀ **March 30**
Color: White

Moon Sign: Virgo
Moon Phase: Second Quarter

♄ **March 31**
Color: Gray

Moon Sign: Virgo
Moon Phase: Second Quarter

April 2007

Ancient African Art Revered

Ancient African art sites in Malawi, Tanzania, and Senegal have been recognized as culturally significant, and will be protected by UNESCO through their designation as World Heritage sites. In Malawi, the Chongoni rock art area has the largest concentration of rock art in Central Africa spread over 127 sites. Included are rare farmer rock art specimens and paintings by BaTwa hunter-gatherers from the late Stone Age. Additionally, there are Chewa rock paintings dating from the late Iron Age. In Tanzania, the Kondoa rock art sites include 150 shelters used for rock paintings that depict beliefs, rituals, and cosmological traditions of the societies that dwelled there. The Stone Circles of the Senegambia site in Senegal includes stone circles, tumuli, burial mounds, and latterite pillars. These sites date from 300 BC to AD 1600.

April 1
April Fools' Day
Palm Sunday
Color: Yellow

⊙
Moon Sign: Virgo
Moon Phase: Second Quarter
Moon enters Libra 11:43 am

☽

April 2

Moon Sign: Libra
Moon Phase: Second Quarter
Seed Moon/Full Moon 1:15 pm

Color: Silver

♂

April 3

Moon Sign: Libra
Moon Phase: Third Quarter

Passover begins
Color: Red

☿

April 4

Moon Sign: Libra
Moon Phase: Third Quarter
Moon enters Scorpio 12:35 am

Color: Yellow

♃

April 5

Moon Sign: Scorpio
Moon Phase: Third Quarter

Color: Turquoise

♀

April 6

Moon Sign: Scorpio
Moon Phase: Third Quarter
Moon enters Sagittarius 12:56 pm

Good Friday · Orthodox Good Friday
Color: White

♄

April 7

Moon Sign: Sagittarius
Moon Phase: Third Quarter

Color: Black

☉

April 8

Moon Sign: Sagittarius
Moon Phase: Third Quarter
Moon enters Capricorn 11:36 pm

Easter · Orthodox Easter
Color: Orange

April 9
Color: Lavender

☽

Moon Sign: Capricorn
Moon Phase: Third Quarter

April 10
Passover ends
Color: Red

♂

Moon Sign: Capricorn
Moon Phase: Third Quarter
Fourth Quarter 2:04 pm

April 11
Color: Yellow

☿

Moon Sign: Capricorn
Moon Phase: Fourth Quarter
Moon enters Aquarius 7:23 am

April 12
Cerealia (Roman)
Color: Violet

♃

Moon Sign: Aquarius
Moon Phase: Fourth Quarter

April 13
Color: Pink

♀

Moon Sign: Aquarius
Moon Phase: Fourth Quarter
Moon enters Pisces 11:38 am

April 14
Color: Black

♄

Moon Sign: Pisces
Moon Phase: Fourth Quarter

April 15
Color: Gold

☉

Moon Sign: Pisces
Moon Phase: Fourth Quarter
Moon enters Aries 12:46 pm

☽ **April 16**

Moon Sign: Aries
Moon Phase: Fourth Quarter

Color: White

♂ **April 17**

Moon Sign: Aries
Moon Phase: Fourth Quarter
New Moon 7:36 am
Moon enters Taurus 12:11 pm

Color: Maroon

☿ **April 18**

Moon Sign: Taurus
Moon Phase: First Quarter

Color: Topaz

♃ **April 19**

Moon Sign: Taurus
Moon Phase: First Quarter
Moon enters Gemini 11:51 am

Color: Green

♀ **April 20**

Moon Sign: Gemini
Moon Phase: First Quarter

Drum Festival (Japanese)
Color: Rose

♄ **April 21**

Moon Sign: Gemini
Moon Phase: First Quarter
Moon enters Cancer 1:50 pm

Color: Gray

☉ **April 22**

Moon Sign: Cancer
Moon Phase: First Quarter

Earth Day
Color: Orange

April 23
Color: Ivory

☽

Moon Sign: Cancer
Moon Phase: First Quarter
Moon enters Leo 7:38 pm

April 24
Color: Red

♂

Moon Sign: Leo
Moon Phase: First Quarter
Second Quarter 2:35 am

April 25
Color: Yellow

☿

Moon Sign: Leo
Moon Phase: Second Quarter

April 26
Arbor Day
Color: Purple

♃

Moon Sign: Leo
Moon Phase: Second Quarter
Moon enters Virgo 5:24 am

April 27
Color: Pink

♀

Moon Sign: Virgo
Moon Phase: Second Quarter

April 28
Floralia (Roman)
Color: Blue

♄

Moon Sign: Virgo
Moon Phase: Second Quarter
Moon enters Libra 5:44 pm

April 29
Color: Amber

☉

Moon Sign: Libra
Moon Phase: Second Quarter

May Eve

An ancient Celtic tradition called for hearth fires to be extinguished on May Eve. The next day people carried torches lit from the Beltane bonfires to relight their home fires. The Wiccan Rede that follows lists nine sacred woods used to build the Beltane fires.

Nine woods in the Cauldron go, burn them fast and burn them slow.

Birch wood in the fire goes to represent what the Lady knows.

Oak in the forest, towers with might in the fire it brings the God's insight.

Rowan is a tree of power causing life and magick to flower.

Willows at the waterside stand ready to help us to the Summerland.

Hawthorn is burned to purify and to draw faerie to your eye.

Hazel—the tree of wisdom and learning—adds its strength to the bright fire burning.

White are the flowers of Apple tree that brings us fruits of fertility.

Grapes grow upon the vine giving us both joy and wine.

Fir does mark the evergreen to represent immortality seen.

May 2007

May 1 ♂

Beltane · May Day
Color: Scarlet

Moon Sign: Libra
Moon Phase: Second Quarter
Moon enters Scorpio 6:41 am

May 2 ☿

Color: White

Moon Sign: Scorpio
Moon Phase: Second Quarter
Hare Moon/Full Moon 6:09 am

May 3 ♃

Color: Yellow

Moon Sign: Scorpio
Moon Phase: Third Quarter
Moon enters Sagittarius 6:47 pm

May 4 ♀

Color: Purple

Moon Sign: Sagittarius
Moon Phase: Third Quarter

May 5 ♄

Cinco de Mayo (Mexican)
Color: Brown

Moon Sign: Sagittarius
Moon Phase: Third Quarter

May 6 ☉

Color: Yellow

Moon Sign: Sagittarius
Moon Phase: Third Quarter
Moon enters Capricorn 5:21 am

☽   May 7

Moon Sign: Capricorn
Moon Phase: Third Quarter

Color: Gray

♂   May 8

Moon Sign: Capricorn
Moon Phase: Third Quarter
Moon enters Aquarius 1:48 pm

Color: Red

☿   May 9

Moon Sign: Aquarius
Moon Phase: Third Quarter

Color: Brown

♃   May 10

Moon Sign: Aquarius
Moon Phase: Third Quarter
Fourth Quarter 12:27 am
Moon enters Pisces 7:31 pm

Color: Turquoise

♀   May 11

Moon Sign: Pisces
Moon Phase: Fourth Quarter

Color: Rose

♄   May 12

Moon Sign: Pisces
Moon Phase: Fourth Quarter
Moon enters Aries 10:19 pm

Color: Black

☉   May 13

Moon Sign: Aries
Moon Phase: Fourth Quarter

Mother's Day
Color: Orange

May 14
Color: Ivory

☽

Moon Sign: Aries
Moon Phase: Fourth Quarter
Moon enters Taurus 10:48 pm

May 15
Color: White

♂

Moon Sign: Taurus
Moon Phase: Fourth Quarter

May 16
Color: Yellow

☿

Moon Sign: Taurus
Moon Phase: Fourth Quarter
New Moon 3:27 pm
Moon enters Gemini 10:34 pm

May 17
Color: Green

♃

Moon Sign: Gemini
Moon Phase: First Quarter

May 18
Color: Coral

♀

Moon Sign: Gemini
Moon Phase: First Quarter
Moon enters Cancer 11:38 pm

May 19
Color: Indigo

♄

Moon Sign: Cancer
Moon Phase: First Quarter

May 20
Color: Orange

☉

Moon Sign: Cancer
Moon Phase: First Quarter

☽

Moon Sign: Cancer
Moon Phase: First Quarter
Moon enters Leo 3:56 am
Sun enters Gemini 6:12 am

May 21
Color: Silver

♂

Moon Sign: Leo
Moon Phase: First Quarter

May 22
Color: Black

☿

Moon Sign: Leo
Moon Phase: First Quarter
Moon enters Virgo 12:26 pm
Second Quarter 5:02 pm

May 23
Shavuot
Color: White

♃

Moon Sign: Virgo
Moon Phase: Second Quarter

May 24
Color: Crimson

♀

Moon Sign: Virgo
Moon Phase: Second Quarter

May 25
Lady Godiva's Day
Color: Rose

♄

Moon Sign: Virgo
Moon Phase: Second Quarter
Moon enters Libra 12:16 am

May 26
Color: Gray

☉

Moon Sign: Libra
Moon Phase: Second Quarter

May 27
Color: Yellow

May 28 ☽

Memorial Day (observed)
Color: Lavender

Moon Sign: Libra
Moon Phase: Second Quarter
Moon enters Scorpio 1:11 pm

May 29 ♂

Color: Gray

Moon Sign: Scorpio
Moon Phase: Second Quarter

May 30 ☿

Color: Brown

Moon Sign: Scorpio
Moon Phase: Second Quarter

May 31 ♃

Color: Violet

Moon Sign: Scorpio
Moon Phase: Second Quarter
Moon enters Sagittarius 1:06 am
Blue Moon/Full Moon 9:04 pm

Blue Moon Weather

In a month with two Full Moons, the second Full Moon is called the Blue Moon, which has been associated with foul weather and storms.

News Items

Adult Version of Hogwart's Opens

Modeled after Hogwarts School of Witchcraft and Wizardry in the Harry Potter books, the Northern Star College of Mystical Studies has opened in Alberta, Canada. The school for adult learners offers programs in herbology, potions, astrology, divination, aromatherapy, flower essences, and mystical studies. Visit www.centercollege-wholistic.ca/ for information.

June 2007

♀	**June 1**
Moon Sign: Sagittarius Moon Phase: Third Quarter	Color: White

♄	**June 2**
Moon Sign: Sagittarius Moon Phase: Third Quarter Moon enters Capricorn 11:09 am	Color: Blue

☉	**June 3**
Moon Sign: Capricorn Moon Phase: Third Quarter	Color: Amber

June 4

☽

Color: White

Moon Sign: Capricorn
Moon Phase: Third Quarter
Moon enters Aquarius 7:15 pm

June 5

♂

Color: Maroon

Moon Sign: Aquarius
Moon Phase: Third Quarter

June 6

☿

Color: Yellow

Moon Sign: Aquarius
Moon Phase: Third Quarter

June 7

♃

Color: Green

Moon Sign: Aquarius
Moon Phase: Third Quarter
Moon enters Pisces 1:24 am

June 8

♀

Color: Violet

Moon Sign: Pisces
Moon Phase: Third Quarter
Fourth Quarter: 7:43 am

June 9

♄

Color: Black

Moon Sign: Pisces
Moon Phase: Fourth Quarter
Moon enters Aries 5:26 am

June 10

☉

Color: Gold

Moon Sign: Aries
Moon Phase: Fourth Quarter

☽   **June 11**
Color: Silver

Moon Sign: Aries
Moon Phase: Fourth Quarter
Moon enters Taurus 7:29 am

♂   **June 12**
Color: Red

Moon Sign: Taurus
Moon Phase: Fourth Quarter

☿   **June 13**
Color: Brown

Moon Sign: Taurus
Moon Phase: Fourth Quarter
Moon enters Gemini 8:24 am

♃   **June 14**
Flag Day
Color: Crimson

Moon Sign: Gemini
Moon Phase: Fourth Quarter
New Moon 11:13 pm

♀   **June 15**
Color: Pink

Moon Sign: Gemini
Moon Phase: First Quarter
Moon enters Cancer 9:45 am

♄   **June 16**
Color: Brown

Moon Sign: Cancer
Moon Phase: First Quarter

☉   **June 17**
Father's Day
Color: Orange

Moon Sign: Cancer
Moon Phase: First Quarter
Moon enters Leo 1:25 pm

June 18
Color: Ivory

☽

Moon Sign: Leo
Moon Phase: First Quarter

June 19
Juneteenth
Color: Red

♂

Moon Sign: Leo
Moon Phase: First Quarter
Moon enters Virgo 8:45 pm

June 20
Color: White

☿

Moon Sign: Virgo
Moon Phase: First Quarter

June 21
Litha · Summer Solstice
Yule · Winter Solstice
    (Southern Hemisphere)
Color: Violet

♃

Moon Sign: Virgo
Moon Phase: First Quarter
Sun enters Cancer 2:06 pm

June 22
Color: Purple

♀

Moon Sign: Virgo
Moon Phase: First Quarter
Moon enters Libra 7:43 am
Second Quarter 9:15 am

June 23
Midsummer Night
Color: Indigo

♄

Moon Sign: Libra
Moon Phase: Second Quarter

June 24
Midsummer Day
Color: Gold

☉

Moon Sign: Libra
Moon Phase: Second Quarter
Moon enters Scorpio 8:26 pm

☽ **June 25**
Color: White

Moon Sign: Scorpio
Moon Phase: Second Quarter

♂ **June 26**
Color: Black

Moon Sign: Scorpio
Moon Phase: Second Quarter

☿ **June 27**
Color: Brown

Moon Sign: Scorpio
Moon Phase: Second Quarter
Moon enters Sagittarius 8:23 am

♃ **June 28**
Color: Green

Moon Sign: Sagittarius
Moon Phase: Second Quarter

♀ **June 29**
Color: White

Moon Sign: Sagittarius
Moon Phase: Second Quarter
Moon enters Capricorn 6:05 pm

♄ **June 30**
Color: Blue

Moon Sign: Capricorn
Moon Phase: Second Quarter
Dyad Moon/Full Moon 9:49 am

News Item

Greek Neo-Pagans Prometheus Bound

Four thousand Neo-Pagans gathered on Mount Olympus and celebrated their annual Prometheus Festival. They conducted rituals and celebrations, and local religious officials said "they were dancing in the meadow, naked." Father Eustathios Kollas, a leader from the Greek Orthodox Church, was quoted as saying: "What these worshippers symbolize, and clearly want, is a return to the monstrous dark delusions of the past. They should be stopped." Regardless of protests from the church communities, the Greek government allowed Neo-Pagans to officially form a cultural association. They eventually hope to be recognized as an official religion.

July 1

Canada Day (Canadian)
Color: Amber

⊙

Moon Sign: Capricorn
Moon Phase: Third Quarter

☽ **July 2**

Color: Silver

Moon Sign: Capricorn
Moon Phase: Third Quarter
Moon enters Aquarius 1:24 am

♂ **July 3**

Color: Scarlet

Moon Sign: Aquarius
Moon Phase: Third Quarter

☿ **July 4**

Independence Day
Color: Topaz

Moon Sign: Aquarius
Moon Phase: Third Quarter
Moon enters Pisces 6:52 am

♃ **July 5**

Color: Turquoise

Moon Sign: Pisces
Moon Phase: Third Quarter

♀ **July 6**

Color: Rose

Moon Sign: Pisces
Moon Phase: Third Quarter
Moon enters Aries 10:56 am

♄ **July 7**

Color: Blue

Moon Sign: Aries
Moon Phase: Third Quarter
Fourth Quarter 12:53 pm

☉ **July 8**

Color: Orange

Moon Sign: Aries
Moon Phase: Fourth Quarter
Moon enters Taurus 1:54 pm

July 9
Color: Lavender

☽

Moon Sign: Taurus
Moon Phase: Fourth Quarter

July 10
Color: White

♂

Moon Sign: Taurus
Moon Phase: Fourth Quarter
Moon enters Gemini 4:10 pm

July 11
Color: Brown

☿

Moon Sign: Gemini
Moon Phase: Fourth Quarter

July 12
Color: Violet

♃

Moon Sign: Gemini
Moon Phase: Fourth Quarter
Moon enters Cancer 6:39 pm

July 13
Color: White

♀

Moon Sign: Cancer
Moon Phase: Fourth Quarter

July 14
Color: Indigo

♄

Moon Sign: Cancer
Moon Phase: Fourth Quarter
New Moon 8:04 am
Moon enters Leo 10:43 pm

July 15
Color: Yellow

☉

Moon Sign: Leo
Moon Phase: First Quarter

☽   **July 16**
Moon Sign: Leo   Color: Ivory
Moon Phase: First Quarter

♂   **July 17**
Moon Sign: Leo   Color: Maroon
Moon Phase: First Quarter
Moon enters Virgo 5:39 am

☿   **July 18**
Moon Sign: Virgo   Color: Topaz
Moon Phase: First Quarter

♃   **July 19**
Moon Sign: Virgo   Color: Crimson
Moon Phase: First Quarter
Moon enters Libra 3:53 pm

♀   **July 20**
Moon Sign: Libra   Color: Rose
Moon Phase: First Quarter

♄   **July 21**
Moon Sign: Libra   Color: Black
Moon Phase: First Quarter

☉   **July 22**
Moon Sign: Libra   Color: Amber
Moon Phase: First Quarter
Second Quarter 2:29 am
Moon enters Scorpio 4:18 am

July 23
Color: White

☽

Moon Sign: Scorpio
Moon Phase: Second Quarter
Sun enters Leo 1:00 am

July 24
Color: Red

♂

Moon Sign: Scorpio
Moon Phase: Second Quarter
Moon enters Sagittarius 4:29 pm

July 25
Color: Yellow

☿

Moon Sign: Sagittarius
Moon Phase: Second Quarter

July 26
Color: Violet

♃

Moon Sign: Sagittarius
Moon Phase: Second Quarter

July 27
Color: Pink

♀

Moon Sign: Sagittarius
Moon Phase: Second Quarter
Moon enters Capricorn 2:21 am

July 28
Color: Gray

♄

Moon Sign: Capricorn
Moon Phase: Second Quarter

July 29
Color: Orange

☉

Moon Sign: Capricorn
Moon Phase: Second Quarter
Moon enters Aquarius 9:13 am
Mead Moon/Full Moon 8:48 pm

☽

Moon Sign: Aquarius
Moon Phase: Third Quarter

♂

Moon Sign: Aquarius
Moon Phase: Third Quarter
Moon enters Pisces 1:40 pm

Strawberry Magic

The roots, leaves, and berries from strawberry plants are used in medicines, beauty treatments, foods, and teas. And let's not forget that the fruit is considered a wonderful aphrodisiac. It's also a fantastic tonic. For a quick facial, rub crushed strawberries on your face (unless you're allergic to them) and leave on for 5 minutes. Rinse with clear water and apply your favorite moisturizer. You can dry strawberry leaves for use throughout the year, and when winter settles around you (or any time you like), pour 1 cup of boiling water over 1 teaspoon of the dried leaves. Steep 10–15 minutes, strain, and sweeten to taste.

August 2007

August 1
Lammas
Color: Brown

☿
Moon Sign: Pisces
Moon Phase: Third Quarter

August 2
Color: Violet

♃
Moon Sign: Pisces
Moon Phase: Third Quarter
Moon enters Aries 4:43 pm

August 3
Color: White

♀
Moon Sign: Aries
Moon Phase: Third Quarter

August 4
Color: Gray

♄
Moon Sign: Aries
Moon Phase: Third Quarter
Moon enters Taurus 7:16 pm

August 5
Color: Gold

☉
Moon Sign: Taurus
Moon Phase: Third Quarter
Fourth Quarter 5:19 pm

☽
August 6
Color: Silver

Moon Sign: Taurus
Moon Phase: Fourth Quarter
Moon enters Gemini 10:01 pm

♂
August 7
Color: White

Moon Sign: Gemini
Moon Phase: Fourth Quarter

☿
August 8
Color: Yellow

Moon Sign: Gemini
Moon Phase: Fourth Quarter

♃
August 9
Color: Violet

Moon Sign: Gemini
Moon Phase: Fourth Quarter
Moon enters Cancer 1:36 am

♀
August 10
Color: Rose

Moon Sign: Cancer
Moon Phase: Fourth Quarter

♄
August 11
Puck Fair (Irish)
Color: Black

Moon Sign: Cancer
Moon Phase: Fourth Quarter
Moon enters Leo 6:42 am

☉
August 12
Color: Yellow

Moon Sign: Leo
Moon Phase: Fourth Quarter
New Moon 7:02 pm

August 13
Color: White

☽

Moon Sign: Leo
Moon Phase: First Quarter
Moon enters Virgo 2:03 pm

Monday

August 14
Color: Red

♂

Moon Sign: Virgo
Moon Phase: First Quarter

Tuesday

August 15
Color: Brown

☿

Moon Sign: Virgo
Moon Phase: First Quarter

Wednesday

August 16
Color: Crimson

♃

Moon Sign: Virgo
Moon Phase: First Quarter
Moon enters Libra 12:04 am

Thursday

August 17
Color: Pink

♀

Moon Sign: Libra
Moon Phase: First Quarter

Friday

August 18
Color: Blue

♄

Moon Sign: Libra
Moon Phase: First Quarter
Moon enters Scorpio 12:13 pm

Saturday

August 19
Color: Yellow

☉

Moon Sign: Scorpio
Moon Phase: First Quarter

Sunday

☽

August 20
Color: Ivory

Moon Sign: Scorpio
Moon Phase: First Quarter
Second Quarter 7:54 pm

♂

August 21
Color: Black

Moon Sign: Scorpio
Moon Phase: Second Quarter
Moon enters Sagittarius 12:44 am

☿

August 22
Color: Yellow

Moon Sign: Sagittarius
Moon Phase: Second Quarter

♃

August 23
Color: Turquoise

Moon Sign: Sagittarius
Moon Phase: Second Quarter
Sun enters Virgo 8:08 am
Moon enters Capricorn 11:20 am

♀

August 24
Color: Rose

Moon Sign: Capricorn
Moon Phase: Second Quarter

♄

August 25
Color: Gray

Moon Sign: Capricorn
Moon Phase: Second Quarter
Moon enters Aquarius 6:35 pm

☉

August 26
Color: Amber

Moon Sign: Aquarius
Moon Phase: Second Quarter

August 27
Color: Silver

☽

Moon Sign: Aquarius
Moon Phase: Second Quarter
Moon enters Pisces 10:34 pm

August 28
Color: Maroon

♂

Moon Sign: Pisces
Moon Phase: Second Quarter
Corn Moon/Full Moon 6:35 am

August 29
Color: Brown

☿

Moon Sign: Pisces
Moon Phase: Third Quarter

August 30
Color: White

♃

Moon Sign: Pisces
Moon Phase: Third Quarter
Moon enters Aries 12:24 am

August 31
Color: Coral

♀

Moon Sign: Aries
Moon Phase: Third Quarter

News Item

Proud to be Pagan

The Pagan Pride Project sponsors public events every September. Public gatherings (where Pagans can network and celebrate Autumn Equinox), are organized by coordinators and local Pagan groups. Events include a charitable activity to share the abundance of harvest and Equinox, and information sharing. Pagans also conduct a media campaign for the events to present clear information about Pagans to the larger community.

♄

September 1

Color: Black

Moon Sign: Aries
Moon Phase: Third Quarter
Moon enters Taurus 1:35 am

☉

September 2

Color: Gold

Moon Sign: Taurus
Moon Phase: Third Quarter

September 3
Labor Day (observed)
Color: Lavender

☽

Moon Sign: Taurus
Moon Phase: Third Quarter
Moon enters Gemini 3:30 am
Fourth Quarter 10:32 pm

September 4
Color: White

♂

Moon Sign: Gemini
Moon Phase: Fourth Quarter

September 5
Color: Yellow

☿

Moon Sign: Gemini
Moon Phase: Fourth Quarter
Moon enters Cancer 7:08 am

September 6
Color: Purple

♃

Moon Sign: Cancer
Moon Phase: Fourth Quarter

September 7
Color: Rose

♀

Moon Sign: Cancer
Moon Phase: Fourth Quarter
Moon enters Leo 12:59 pm

September 8
Color: Black

♄

Moon Sign: Leo
Moon Phase: Fourth Quarter

September 9
Color: Yellow

☉

Moon Sign: Leo
Moon Phase: Fourth Quarter
Moon enters Virgo 9:10 pm

☽

September 10
Color: Gray

Moon Sign: Virgo
Moon Phase: Fourth Quarter

♂

September 11
Color: Red

Moon Sign: Virgo
Moon Phase: Fourth Quarter
New Moon 8:44 am

☿

September 12
Color: Brown

Moon Sign: Virgo
Moon Phase: First Quarter
Moon enters Libra 7:31 am

♃

September 13
Ramadan begins
Rosh Hashanah (Jewish New Year)
Color: Green

Moon Sign: Libra
Moon Phase: First Quarter

♀

September 14
Color: Pink

Moon Sign: Libra
Moon Phase: First Quarter
Moon enters Scorpio 7:37 pm

♄

September 15
Birthday of the Moon (Chinese)
Color: Blue

Moon Sign: Scorpio
Moon Phase: First Quarter

☉

September 16
Color: Amber

Moon Sign: Scorpio
Moon Phase: First Quarter

September 17
Color: Ivory

☽

Moon Sign: Scorpio
Moon Phase: First Quarter
Moon enters Sagittarius 8:21 am

September 18
Color: Black

♂

Moon Sign: Sagittarius
Moon Phase: First Quarter

September 19
Color: White

☿

Moon Sign: Sagittarius
Moon Phase: First Quarter
Second Quarter 12:48 pm
Moon enters Capricorn 7:51 pm

September 20
Color: Violet

♃

Moon Sign: Capricorn
Moon Phase: Second Quarter

September 21
Color: Coral

♀

Moon Sign: Capricorn
Moon Phase: Second Quarter

September 22
Yom Kippur
Color: Gray

♄

Moon Sign: Capricorn
Moon Phase: Second Quarter
Moon enters Aquarius 4:18 am

September 23
Mabon · Fall Equinox
Ostara · Spring Equinox
   (Southern Hemisphere)
Color: Orange

☉

Moon Sign: Aquarius
Moon Phase: Second Quarter
Sun enters Libra 5:51 am

☽   **September 24**

Color: Gray

Moon Sign: Aquarius
Moon Phase: Second Quarter
Moon enters Pisces 8:55 am

♂   **September 25**

Color: Red

Moon Sign: Pisces
Moon Phase: Second Quarter

☿   **September 26**

Color: Topaz

Moon Sign: Pisces
Moon Phase: Second Quarter
Moon enters Aries 10:22 am
Harvest Moon/Full Moon 3:45 pm

♃   **September 27**

Sukkot begins
Color: Purple

Moon Sign: Aries
Moon Phase: Third Quarter

♀   **September 28**

Color: White

Moon Sign: Aries
Moon Phase: Third Quarter
Moon enters Taurus 10:17 am

♄   **September 29**

Color: Brown

Moon Sign: Taurus
Moon Phase: Third Quarter

☉   **September 30**

Color: Gold

Moon Sign: Taurus
Moon Phase: Third Quarter
Moon enters Gemini 10:34 am

October 2007

October 1
Color: White

☽

Moon Sign: Gemini
Moon Phase: Third Quarter

October 2
Color: Red

♂

Moon Sign: Gemini
Moon Phase: Third Quarter
Moon enters Cancer 12:57 pm

October 3
Sukkot ends
Color: Brown

☿

Moon Sign: Cancer
Moon Phase: Third Quarter
Fourth Quarter 6:06 am

October 4
Color: Violet

♃

Moon Sign: Cancer
Moon Phase: Fourth Quarter
Moon enters Leo 6:27 pm

October 5
Color: Pink

♀

Moon Sign: Leo
Moon Phase: Fourth Quarter

October 6
Color: Black

♄

Moon Sign: Leo
Moon Phase: Fourth Quarter

October 7
Color: Amber

☉

Moon Sign: Leo
Moon Phase: Fourth Quarter
Moon enters Virgo 3:03 am

☽ **October 8**

Columbus Day (observed)
Color: Lavender

Moon Sign: Virgo
Moon Phase: Fourth Quarter

♂ **October 9**

Color: White

Moon Sign: Virgo
Moon Phase: Fourth Quarter
Moon enters Libra 1:57 pm

☿ **October 10**

Color: Yellow

Moon Sign: Libra
Moon Phase: Fourth Quarter

♃ **October 11**

Color: Turquoise

Moon Sign: Libra
Moon Phase: Fourth Quarter
New Moon 1:01 am

♀ **October 12**

Color: Rose

Moon Sign: Libra
Moon Phase: First Quarter
Moon enters Scorpio 2:13 am

♄ **October 13**

Ramadan ends
Color: Indigo

Moon Sign: Scorpio
Moon Phase: First Quarter

☉ **October 14**

Color: Orange

Moon Sign: Scorpio
Moon Phase: First Quarter
Moon enters Sagittarius 2:58 pm

October 15
Color: White

☽

Moon Sign: Sagittarius
Moon Phase: First Quarter

October 16
Color: Red

♂

Moon Sign: Sagittarius
Moon Phase: First Quarter

October 17
Color: Brown

☿

Moon Sign: Sagittarius
Moon Phase: First Quarter
Moon enters Capricorn 3:03 am

October 18
Color: Violet

♃

Moon Sign: Capricorn
Moon Phase: First Quarter

October 19
Color: White

♀

Moon Sign: Capricorn
Moon Phase: First Quarter
Second Quarter 4:33 am
Moon enters Aquarius 12:52 pm

October 20
Color: Blue

♄

Moon Sign: Aquarius
Moon Phase: Second Quarter

October 21
Color: Yellow

☉

Moon Sign: Aquarius
Moon Phase: Second Quarter
Moon enters Pisces 7:02 pm

☽   **October 22**
Moon Sign: Pisces   Color: Silver
Moon Phase: Second Quarter

♂   **October 23**
Moon Sign: Pisces   Color: Scarlet
Moon Phase: Second Quarter
Sun enters Scorpio 3:15 pm
Moon enters Aries 9:24 pm

☿   **October 24**
Moon Sign: Aries   Color: White
Moon Phase: Second Quarter

♃   **October 25**
Moon Sign: Aries   Color: Purple
Moon Phase: Second Quarter
Moon enters Taurus 9:07 pm

♀   **October 26**
Moon Sign: Taurus   Color: Coral
Moon Phase: Second Quarter
Blood Moon/Full Moon 12:51 am

♄   **October 27**
Moon Sign: Taurus   Color: Black
Moon Phase: Third Quarter
Moon enters Gemini 8:11 pm

☉   **October 28**
Moon Sign: Gemini   Color: Amber
Moon Phase: Third Quarter

October 29

☽

Color: Ivory

Moon Sign: Gemini
Moon Phase: Third Quarter
Moon enters Cancer 8:49 pm

October 30

♂

Color: Black

Moon Sign: Cancer
Moon Phase: Third Quarter

October 31

☿

Halloween · Samhain
Beltane (Southern Hemisphere)
Color: Yellow

Moon Sign: Cancer
Moon Phase: Third Quarter

Psychologist Accused of Witchcraft

Attorneys for Dr. Letitia Libman, who was accused of practicing witchcraft on her patients in Geneva, Illinois, called the claims "scripted." The lawsuit for $1 million, filed on behalf of a former patient, sued the Delnow Community Hospital in Geneva, Illinois, where Libman ran the St. Charles treatment facility. Though Libman has remained silent since she was charged, her attorneys released a statement denying the allegations. The lawsuits, which make more than 100 accusations, claim Libman practiced witchcraft on each of the alleged victims. The lawyer's statement also intoned that media coverage of the lawsuits is a "disservice to the local community," and "creates bias and prejudgement."

This Witch Doesn't Spook Easily

After being spit on and having had Bibles thrown at her, Pagan entrepreneur Bronwyn Cabot Butler said she isn't easily spooked. Butler moved from Wintersville, Ohio, where these incidents occurred, to Bethlehem in the Lehigh Valley of Pennsylvania, where she now operates Ostara, a witchcraft boutique.

Named after a the holiday that celebrates the start of spring and new beginnings, Ostara is a new beginning for Butler. Bethlehem, with many practicing Neo-Pagans, is a lot more accepting of her and her business. Celebrating her new location, Butler has designed a "Bethlehem star spell," combining a blend of prosperity herbs and a large star to hang in a prominent spot. The star used is an original Bethlehem star, which was historically constructed to help attract business to the area.

November 2007

News Item

Fallen Pagan Hero Honored

The first Pentacle to appear in the U.S. Department of Veterans Affairs memorial plaque was fought for, and won by, Roberta Stewart, widow of Sgt. Patrick Stewart. Stewart was killed in Afghanistan. Initially, the VA refused to allow a pentacle on the memorial plaque because they don't recognize Wicca as a religion. But Stewart's widow petitioned the Nevada Attorney General's Office, which concluded that federal officials have no authority over the state veteran's cemetery.

November 1   ♃
All Saints' Day   Moon Sign: Cancer
Color: Turquoise   Moon Phase: Third Quarter
                                Moon enters Leo 12:48 am
                                   Fourth Quarter 5:18 pm

November 2   ♀
Color: White   Moon Sign: Leo
                                Moon Phase: Fourth Quarter

November 3   ♄
Color: Gray   Moon Sign: Leo
                                Moon Phase: Fourth Quarter
                                Moon enters Virgo 8:44 am

November 4   ☉
Daylight Saving Time ends, 2 am   Moon Sign: Virgo
Color: Orange   Moon Phase: Fourth Quarter

☽

Moon Sign: Virgo
Moon Phase: Fourth Quarter
Moon enters Libra 6:47 pm

November 5
Color: Silver

♂

Moon Sign: Libra
Moon Phase: Fourth Quarter

November 6
Election Day
Color: White

☿

Moon Sign: Libra
Moon Phase: Fourth Quarter

November 7
Color: Brown

♃

Moon Sign: Libra
Moon Phase: Fourth Quarter
Moon enters Scorpio 7:18 am

November 8
Color: Violet

♀

Moon Sign: Scorpio
Moon Phase: Fourth Quarter
New Moon 6:03 pm

November 9
Color: Coral

♄

Moon Sign: Scorpio
Moon Phase: First Quarter
Moon enters Sagittarius 7:59 pm

November 10
Color: Black

☉

Moon Sign: Sagittarius
Moon Phase: First Quarter

November 11
Veterans Day
Color: Amber

November 12 ☽
Color: Lavender

Moon Sign: Sagittarius
Moon Phase: First Quarter

November 13 ♂
Color: Red

Moon Sign: Sagittarius
Moon Phase: First Quarter
Moon enters Capricorn 8:00 am

November 14 ☿
Color: White

Moon Sign: Capricorn
Moon Phase: First Quarter

November 15 ♃
Color: Green

Moon Sign: Capricorn
Moon Phase: First Quarter
Moon enters Aquarius 6:30 pm

November 16 ♀
Color: Coral

Moon Sign: Aquarius
Moon Phase: First Quarter

November 17 ♄
Color: Indigo

Moon Sign: Aquarius
Moon Phase: First Quarter
Second Quarter 5:32 pm

November 18 ☉
Color: Amber

Moon Sign: Aquarius
Moon Phase: Second Quarter
Moon enters Pisces 2:14 am

☽

November 19
Color: Ivory

Moon Sign: Pisces
Moon Phase: Second Quarter

♂

November 20
Color: Black

Moon Sign: Pisces
Moon Phase: Second Quarter
Moon enters Aries 6:24 am

☿

November 21
Color: Topaz

Moon Sign: Aries
Moon Phase: Second Quarter

♃

November 22
Thanksgiving Day
Color: Purple

Moon Sign: Aries
Moon Phase: Second Quarter
Moon enters Taurus 7:18 am
Sun enters Sagittarius 11:50 am

♀

November 23
Color: Rose

Moon Sign: Taurus
Moon Phase: Second Quarter

♄

November 24
Color: Black

Moon Sign: Taurus
Moon Phase: Second Quarter
Moon enters Gemini 6:29 am
Snow Moon/Full Moon 9:30 am

☉

November 25
Color: Gold

Moon Sign: Gemini
Moon Phase: Third Quarter

November 26
Color: White

☽

Moon Sign: Gemini
Moon Phase: Third Quarter
Moon enters Cancer 6:07 am

November 27
Color: Scarlet

♂

Moon Sign: Cancer
Moon Phase: Third Quarter

November 28
Color: Brown

☿

Moon Sign: Cancer
Moon Phase: Third Quarter
Moon enters Leo 8:23 am

November 29
Color: Turquoise

♃

Moon Sign: Leo
Moon Phase: Third Quarter

November 30
Color: Purple

♀

Moon Sign: Leo
Moon Phase: Third Quarter
Moon enters Virgo 2:44 pm

December 2007

♄
Moon Sign: Virgo
Moon Phase: Third Quarter
Fourth Quarter 7:44 am

December 1
Color: Gray

☉
Moon Sign: Virgo
Moon Phase: Fourth Quarter

December 2
Color: Indigo

December 3
Color: Silver

☽

Moon Sign: Virgo
Moon Phase: Fourth Quarter
Moon enters Libra 1:01 am

December 4
Color: Black

♂

Moon Sign: Libra
Moon Phase: Fourth Quarter

December 5
Hanukkah begins
Color: White

☿

Moon Sign: Libra
Moon Phase: Fourth Quarter
Moon enters Scorpio 1:31 pm

December 6
Color: Crimson

♃

Moon Sign: Scorpio
Moon Phase: Fourth Quarter

December 7
Color: Rose

♀

Moon Sign: Scorpio
Moon Phase: Fourth Quarter

December 8
Color: Brown

♄

Moon Sign: Scorpio
Moon Phase: Fourth Quarter
Moon enters Sagittarius 2:11 am

December 9
Color: Orange

☉

Moon Sign: Sagittarius
Moon Phase: Fourth Quarter
New Moon 12:40 pm

☽ **December 10**
Color: Lavender
Moon Sign: Sagittarius
Moon Phase: First Quarter
Moon enters Capricorn 1:50 pm

♂ **December 11**
Color: Maroon
Moon Sign: Capricorn
Moon Phase: First Quarter

☿ **December 12**
Hanukkah ends
Color: Yellow
Moon Sign: Capricorn
Moon Phase: First Quarter

♃ **December 13**
Color: Green
Moon Sign: Capricorn
Moon Phase: First Quarter
Moon enters Aquarius 12:01 am

♀ **December 14**
Color: Pink
Moon Sign: Aquarius
Moon Phase: First Quarter

♄ **December 15**
Color: Blue
Moon Sign: Aquarius
Moon Phase: First Quarter
Moon enters Pisces 8:15 am

☉ **December 16**
Color: Gold
Moon Sign: Pisces
Moon Phase: First Quarter

December 17

Saturnalia (Roman)
Color: Silver

☽

Moon Sign: Pisces
Moon Phase: First Quarter
Second Quarter 5:17 am
Moon enters Aries 1:52 pm

December 18

Color: White

♂

Moon Sign: Aries
Moon Phase: Second Quarter

December 19

Color: Brown

☿

Moon Sign: Aries
Moon Phase: Second Quarter
Moon enters Taurus 4:38 pm

December 20

Color: Turquoise

♃

Moon Sign: Taurus
Moon Phase: Second Quarter

December 21

Color: Coral

♀

Moon Sign: Taurus
Moon Phase: Second Quarter
Moon enters Gemini 5:14 pm

December 22

Yule · Winter Solstice
Litha · Summer Solstice
  (Southern Hemisphere)
Color: Indigo

♄

Moon Sign: Gemini
Moon Phase: Second Quarter
Sun enters Capricorn 1:08 am

December 23

Color: Gold

☉

Moon Sign: Gemini
Moon Phase: Second Quarter
Moon enters Cancer 5:18 pm
Oak Moon/Full Moon 8:15 pm

☽

Moon Sign: Cancer
Moon Phase: Third Quarter

December 24
Christmas Eve
Color: Ivory

♂

Moon Sign: Cancer
Moon Phase: Third Quarter
Moon enters Leo 6:52 pm

December 25
Christmas Day
Color: Scarlet

☿

Moon Sign: Leo
Moon Phase: Third Quarter

December 26
Kwanzaa begins
Color: Topaz

♃

Moon Sign: Leo
Moon Phase: Third Quarter
Moon enters Virgo 11:44 pm

December 27
Color: White

♀

Moon Sign: Virgo
Moon Phase: Third Quarter

December 28
Color: Purple

♄

Moon Sign: Virgo
Moon Phase: Third Quarter

December 29
Color: Black

☉

Moon Sign: Virgo
Moon Phase: Third Quarter
Moon enters Libra 8:37 am

December 30
Color: Amber

December 31
New Year's Eve
Color: White

☽

Moon Sign: Libra
Moon Phase: Third Quarter
Fourth Quarter 2:51 am

News Item

Protecting Indigenous Religious Rites

When Russian Vitaly Tanakov wrote a book dedi-cated to the traditions and religion of the Mari, a Finno-Ugric people from the region, he did so to celebrate his heredity. Tanakov is a descendant of ancient priests. But Russian authorities viewed the book, titled *The Priest Speaks*, as violating the Russian constitution, and put Tanakov on trial for allegedly inciting religious, national, social, and linguistic hatred. Experts who analyzed the book said the charges were groundless. Human rights activists worry that if Tanakov is sentenced for describing the Mari national characteristics in his book, the trial will outlaw thousands of the people in the republic for speaking their own language, practicing their own religion, and performing their religious rites.

January 2008
Leap Year

♂

Moon Sign: Libra
Moon Phase: Fourth Quarter
Moon enters Scorpio 8:32 pm

January 1
New Year's Day · Kwanzaa ends
Color: Red

☿

Moon Sign: Scorpio
Moon Phase: Fourth Quarter

January 2
Color: Yellow

♃

Moon Sign: Scorpio
Moon Phase: Fourth Quarter

January 3
Color: Green

♀

Moon Sign: Scorpio
Moon Phase: Fourth Quarter
Moon enters Sagittarius 9:13 am

January 4
Color: White

♄

Moon Sign: Sagittarius
Moon Phase: Fourth Quarter

January 5
Color: Gray

☉

Moon Sign: Sagittarius
Moon Phase: Fourth Quarter
Moon enters Capricorn 8:43 pm

January 6
Color: Orange

January 7
Color: Gray

☽

Moon Sign: Capricorn
Moon Phase: Fourth Quarter

January 8
Color: Scarlet

♂

Moon Sign: Capricorn
Moon Phase: Fourth Quarter
New Moon 6:37 am

January 9
Color: Yellow

☿

Moon Sign: Capricorn
Moon Phase: First Quarter
Moon enters Aquarius 6:13 am

January 10
Color: Violet

♃

Moon Sign: Aquarius
Moon Phase: First Quarter

January 11
Color: White

♀

Moon Sign: Aquarius
Moon Phase: First Quarter
Moon enters Pisces 1:44 pm

January 12
Color: Brown

♄

Moon Sign: Pisces
Moon Phase: First Quarter

January 13
Color: Yellow

☉

Moon Sign: Pisces
Moon Phase: First Quarter
Moon enters Aries 7:23 pm

Monday

Tuesday

Wednesday

Thursday

Friday

Saturday

Sunday

☽

Moon Sign: Aries
Moon Phase: First Quarter

January 14
Color: Lavender

♂

Moon Sign: Aries
Moon Phase: First Quarter
Second Quarter 2:46 pm
Moon enters Taurus 11:13 pm

January 15
Color: White

☿

Moon Sign: Taurus
Moon Phase: Second Quarter

January 16
Apprentices' Day
Color: Brown

♃

Moon Sign: Taurus
Moon Phase: Second Quarter

January 17
Color: Purple

♀

Moon Sign: Taurus
Moon Phase: Second Quarter
Moon enters Gemini 1:30 am

January 18
Color: Coral

♄

Moon Sign: Gemini
Moon Phase: Second Quarter

January 19
Color: Gray

☉

Moon Sign: Gemini
Moon Phase: Second Quarter
Moon enters Cancer 3:05 am
Sun enters Aquarius 11:43 am

January 20
Color: Orange

January 21
Martin Luther King, Jr.'s birthday (observed)
Color: Silver

☽

Moon Sign: Cancer
Moon Phase: Second Quarter

January 22
Color: Red

♂

Moon Sign: Cancer
Moon Phase: Second Quarter
Moon enters Leo 5:20 am
Wolf Moon/Full Moon 8:35 am

January 23
Color: White

☿

Moon Sign: Leo
Moon Phase: Third Quarter

January 24
Color: Green

♃

Moon Sign: Leo
Moon Phase: Third Quarter
Moon enters Virgo 9:48 am

January 25
Color: Pink

♀

Moon Sign: Virgo
Moon Phase: Third Quarter

January 26
Color: Black

♄

Moon Sign: Virgo
Moon Phase: Third Quarter
Moon enters Libra 5:35 pm

January 27
Color: Yellow

☉

Moon Sign: Libra
Moon Phase: Third Quarter

☽	**January 28**
Moon Sign: Libra	Color: Amber
Moon Phase: Third Quarter	

♂	**January 29**
Moon Sign: Libra	Color: Ivory
Moon Phase: Third Quarter	
Moon enters Scorpio 4:35 am	

☿	**January 30**
Moon Sign: Scorpio	Color: Maroon
Moon Phase: Third Quarter	
Fourth Quarter 12:03 am	

♃	**January 31**
Moon Sign: Scorpio	Color: Yellow
Moon Phase: Fourth Quarter	
Moon enters Sagittarius 5:08 am	

News Item

Sacrifice Blamed on Pagans

In County Wicklow, Ireland, the Irish Society for the Prevention of Cruelty to Animals investigated an incident. Apparently, in the village of Enniskerry, a dog was nailed to a cross and left to die. The ISPCA said the incident wasn't immediately reported. By the time they arrived the dog had been bled dry on the home-made altar. Some people have claimed that "Pagans" did it. Local Pagans are outraged, saying crosses, nails, and sacrifice are not part of their spiritual practice. They suggested the ISPCA look to some other local group who uses these symbols commonly in their spiritual practices.

February 2008

February 1
St. Brigid's Day (Irish)
Color: Purple

♀

Moon Sign: Sagittarius
Moon Phase: Fourth Quarter

February 2
Imbolc · Groundhog Day
Color: Blue

♄

Moon Sign: Sagittarius
Moon Phase: Fourth Quarter

February 3
Color: Gold

☉

Moon Sign: Sagittarius
Moon Phase: Fourth Quarter
Moon enters Capricorn 4:52 am

☽

February 4

Color: Silver

Moon Sign: Capricorn
Moon Phase: Fourth Quarter

♂

February 5

Mardi Gras
Color: Black

Moon Sign: Capricorn
Moon Phase: Fourth Quarter
Moon enters Aquarius 2:10 pm

☿

February 6

Ash Wednesday
Color: Topaz

Moon Sign: Aquarius
Moon Phase: Fourth Quarter
New Moon 10:44 pm

♃

February 7

Color: Violet

Moon Sign: Aquarius
Moon Phase: First Quarter
Moon enters Pisces 8:46 pm

♀

February 8

Color: White

Moon Sign: Pisces
Moon Phase: First Quarter

♄

February 9

Color: Brown

Moon Sign: Pisces
Moon Phase: First Quarter

☉

February 10

Color: Yellow

Moon Sign: Pisces
Moon Phase: First Quarter
Moon enters Aries 1:17 am

February 11
Color: Ivory

☽

Moon Sign: Aries
Moon Phase: First Quarter

February 12
Color: White

♂

Moon Sign: Aries
Moon Phase: First Quarter
Moon enters Taurus 4:34 am

February 13
Color: Brown

☿

Moon Sign: Taurus
Moon Phase: First Quarter
Second Quarter 10:33 pm

February 14
Valentine's Day
Color: Turquoise

♃

Moon Sign: Taurus
Moon Phase: Second Quarter
Moon enters Gemini 7:19 am

February 15
Color: Coral

♀

Moon Sign: Gemini
Moon Phase: Second Quarter

February 16
Color: Indigo

♄

Moon Sign: Gemini
Moon Phase: Second Quarter
Moon enters Cancer 10:12 am

February 17
Color: Amber

☉

Moon Sign: Cancer
Moon Phase: Second Quarter

☽

Moon Sign: Cancer
Moon Phase: Second Quarter
Moon enters Leo 1:51 pm

February 18
Presidents' Day (observed)
Color: Gray

♂

Moon Sign: Leo
Moon Phase: Second Quarter
Sun enters Pisces 1:49 am

February 19
Color: Black

☿

Moon Sign: Leo
Moon Phase: Second Quarter
Moon enters Virgo 7:06 pm
Storm Moon/Full Moon 10:30 pm

February 20
Color: Yellow

♃

Moon Sign: Virgo
Moon Phase: Third Quarter

February 21
Ash Wednesday
Color: Violet

♀

Moon Sign: Virgo
Moon Phase: Third Quarter

February 22
Color: Green

♄

Moon Sign: Virgo
Moon Phase: Third Quarter
Moon enters Libra 2:44 am

February 23
Color: Brown

☉

Moon Sign: Libra
Moon Phase: Third Quarter

February 24
Color: Orange

February 25

Color: Ivory

☽

Moon Sign: Libra
Moon Phase: Third Quarter
Moon enters Scorpio 1:05 pm

February 26

Mardi Gras (Fat Tuesday)
Color: Maroon

♂

Moon Sign: Scorpio
Moon Phase: Third Quarter

February 27

Color: White

☿

Moon Sign: Scorpio
Moon Phase: Third Quarter

February 28

Color: Green

♃

Moon Sign: Scorpio
Moon Phase: Third Quarter
Moon enters Sagittarius 1:22 am
Fourth Quarter 9:18 pm

February 29

Leap Day
Color: Pink

♀

Moon Sign: Sagittarius
Moon Phase: Fourth Quarter

March 2008

♄

Moon Sign: Sagittarius
Moon Phase: Fourth Quarter
Moon enters Capricorn 1:33 pm

March 1
Color: Gray

☉

Moon Sign: Capricorn
Moon Phase: Fourth Quarter

March 2
Color: Amber

March 3
Color: Gray

☽

Moon Sign: Capricorn
Moon Phase: Fourth Quarter
Moon enters Aquarius 11:24 pm

March 4
Color: Red

♂

Moon Sign: Aquarius
Moon Phase: Fourth Quarter

March 5
Color: Topaz

☿

Moon Sign: Aquarius
Moon Phase: Fourth Quarter

March 6
Color: Crimson

♃

Moon Sign: Aquarius
Moon Phase: Fourth Quarter
Moon enters Pisces 5:53 am

March 7
Color: Rose

♀

Moon Sign: Pisces
Moon Phase: Fourth Quarter
New Moon 12:14 am

March 8
International Women's Day
Color: Blue

♄

Moon Sign: Pisces
Moon Phase: First Quarter
Moon enters Aries 9:23 am

March 9
Daylight Saving Time begins, 2:00 am
Color: Yellow

☉

Moon Sign: Aries
Moon Phase: First Quarter

☽

Moon Sign: Aries
Moon Phase: First Quarter
Moon enters Taurus 12:13 pm

March 10

Color: Silver

♂

Moon Sign: Taurus
Moon Phase: First Quarter

March 11

Color: Black

☿

Moon Sign: Taurus
Moon Phase: First Quarter
Moon enters Gemini 1:54 pm

March 12

Color: Brown

♃

Moon Sign: Gemini
Moon Phase: First Quarter

March 13

Color: Violet

♀

Moon Sign: Gemini
Moon Phase: First Quarter
Second Quarter 6:45 am
Moon enters Cancer 4:37 pm

March 14

Color: White

♄

Moon Sign: Cancer
Moon Phase: Second Quarter

March 15

Color: Indigo

☉

Moon Sign: Cancer
Moon Phase: Second Quarter
Moon enters Leo 9:04 pm

March 16

Palm Sunday
Color: Amber

March 17

St. Patrick's Day
Color: Gray

☽

Moon Sign: Leo
Moon Phase: Second Quarter

March 18

Color: Red

♂

Moon Sign: Leo
Moon Phase: Second Quarter

March 19

Color: Yellow

☿

Moon Sign: Leo
Moon Phase: Second Quarter
Moon enters Virgo 3:25 am

March 20

Ostara · Spring Equinox
Mabon · Autumnal Equinox
 (Southern Hemisphere)
Color: Turquoise

♃

Moon Sign: Virgo
Moon Phase: Second Quarter
Sun enters Aries 1:48 am

News Item

Urban Tree of the Year

The Bur oak was named tree of the year in 2001
by members of the Society for Municipal Arborists (SMA).
It was chosen for its tolerance of urban environments, cold,
storms, and drought, and for its beauty in summer or winter.
Reaching eighty feet or more, the Bur oak is not ideally suited
to small urban and city lots, but it does well in parks and
places where it has room to spread its roots and branches.

Sweep Me Away!

Tips & suggestions
for Wiccans & Pagans
who wander through
the wide & wondrous
world

Stay Connected Anywhere

by Taylor Ellwood

Feeling connected to other people and to our environment is an essential human need. Without that sense of connection it's easy to feel isolated, lost, and depressed. A year ago I moved from the Midwest to Seattle, Washington; from what was familiar to a place that was totally new. We lived with my mate Lupa's relatives for the first two months, and we had some setbacks in finding jobs and a place to live. Indeed, at times, it seemed like we'd been cursed with a hurricane of bad luck.

I became a victim of job hunting and feeling homeless. A depression set in and I couldn't shake it. My daily practice of shielding and protection rituals fell off.

Today, I know at least some of the setbacks I experienced were brought on by the negativity I felt toward my new circumstances. I didn't feel grounded in my new environment. In a way, I really resented being in Seattle. I felt as if I was being rejected by the environment itself, with no job and no home. In contrast my mate found the job she wanted rather quickly, and she seemed much more welcomed by the area than

The threshold of a home is sacred, for it keeps within what you want, and keeps without that which isn't needed.

I was. Of course, she had a much different attitude than I did about the move. She had anticipated moving out to Seattle and was ready for it emotionally, mentally, and magically.

Our situation came to a head on the day we finally moved into our new home. The flooring was supposed to be renovated. But it wasn't done, due to situations outside of our control. I felt like giving up—like nothing I could do could keep me in this new environment.

And then I got a phone call and the job I wanted. Suddenly, everything had changed. I had a home, and a sense of connection to this new environment. I no longer felt displaced.

The Solution Is Interaction

It took giving up all the feelings I had—positive or negative—about Seattle and everything else in my life, to get me to feel connected. I'd so powerfully let my feelings affect me—color my perception of everything—that I sabotaged myself. Only after all the negativity had come to a head and been expressed and expelled could I actually find success.

A week after I got the job, I started doing my daily rituals, meditating, putting up my shields, and making sure that

everything was right in my inner world so that what manifested outwardly was also right. You know what I realized? I really missed doing those rituals every day. I missed the connection. Those exercises grounded and protected me; they established my sacred space and helped me feel rooted in my new environment.

We do protection and shielding to protect ourselves from the world around us, but sometimes we need to protect ourselves from ourselves. The adage "As within, so without; as above, so below" applies here because our attitudes affect the external realities that we live in. In other words, protection and shielding isn't just protection from whatever is out there, it's also is a balancer and protector from what's within. Finding that internal balance is essential for establishing a sense of connection to your environment, because when you have internal organization you can easily handle what is occurring in the external environment.

Put your inner home in order and you will find a sense of self that is interconnected and no longer adrift in the world.

I do my rituals to establish a sense of peace within myself, to reorder my mental balance so that everything in my subconscious runs smoothly instead of sabotaging me. I do my rituals to put my inner home in order and manifest that home outwardly into the environment I live in, regardless of where I am.

What "Home" Means

When I think of a home, I think of a safe place that provides comfort, warmth, and sustenance. It's a sacred temple, but it's also the center of my reality. Home is where I come back to after a day's work. Home is love, life, reassurance, family, and healing. But home isn't limited to the structure you live in.

Home is your body, which is also your sacred temple. It's your consciousness and subconsciousness. And like any home, what matters is how well you take care of the environment you live in. Energy in a messy home is displaced and disconnected, while the energy in a clean, well-ordered home flows smoothly. The same is true of the inner home of yourself.

When I exercise my body or eat healthy food, I am taking care of the physical home that my soul resides in. I am appreciating it, nurturing it, and cleaning out the toxins. And when I do my daily meditations and rituals, I am cleaning my mental and spiritual home. I am taking care of my inner environment and connecting it to the external environment I live in. I am balancing myself and finding in that balance a way to control and work with my emotions, thoughts, concepts, energy, etc., instead of letting them run wild, and leaving me feeling disconnected with what's around and within me.

The threshold of a home is sacred, for it keeps within what you want, and keeps without that which isn't needed. The rituals of protection and shielding do much the same for a person. They contain and organize what needs to go where, while keeping out intruders. When I visualize my spiritual home, I see a comfortable cottage with a nice porch and a garden. Inside my home, everything is organized and kept in place. Objects inhabit the space they need to be in. And because everything is in its proper place, the energy flows, mental balance is achieved, and each day is manifested in a way that promises success and joy.

How Are You Connected?

Think carefully about your sense of self and how connected it is to the environment and other people. If you're unhappy with what you find, remember that it is your responsibility to make those connections. Put your inner home in order

and you will find a sense of self that is interconnected and no longer adrift in the world.

Go outside, walk around, feel the wind on your face, touch the grass and trees, breathe in the air, and let your sense of self be immersed in the environment around you. Doing this will allow you to connect with nature, which in turn will provide you with grounding.

Don't hesitate to do this indoors, too, as that is also your environment. Look around, and touch things. Take a breath and again immerse your sense of self in your home. Ask yourself why your home is organized the way it is and what that organization (or lack thereof) says about you and your sense of self.

Wicca in the Fast Lane

by Patricia Telesco

When life—the wheel of fate—races out of control, it's natural to brake, close the windows, and seek peace. Something within us yearns to reconnect with stability, and with the sense of our beginning and our end. Our ideologies call us to reclaim and rebuild a functional relationship with sacred powers despite the persistence of change. The ultimate goal is to locate one's path on the road map.

So, exactly how can we obtain good directions into invisible realms? Dante and other creative minds have tried to chart the path to the hereafter, and each version is slightly different. Every world religion has underlying similarities, but the road maps differ.

What's the Eclectic Seeker to Do?

First, we must remind ourselves that a path will never have specific lines or destinations. Each step we take in life's journey changes what we see of the horizon ahead. Therefore, our paths are always developing and evolving.

Second, we need to recognize that being enlightened doesn't mean knowing everything. Actually, the more spiritually aware we become, the more we begin to realize how little we actually know. As much as we might wish otherwise, spiritual awareness doesn't make all the other problems and questions in life disappear.

What spiritually centered living does allow, however, is a way to redefine our journey in a positive, life-affirming manner. Somewhere along the way we lost sight of how to achieve wholeness in body, mind, and spirit, or, how to maintain it when our gears get shifted. So, perhaps we need to make a pit stop—take a moment to redefine spiritual-centeredness and our ideas about the Sacred. Then, deciding what (if any) impact that definition has will determine the way we drive through life.

Life in the Fast Lane

Living in the fast lane only accentuates our confusion. There is rarely enough time for anyone to notice changes, let alone integrate them. In 1950 a housewife was admired and honored. Then, during the ensuing decades, the ideal of the happy homemaker changed, becoming almost a demeaning phrase by the 1980s. But fifteen years later, being a wife, and mother, and a professional, was fashionable again.

People who live in the fast lane of life find that changes are often traumatic, with head-on collisions occurring on the

home front. There must be a better way to navigate the road map of life. Let's take a step back and re-evaluate the lessons we've been given to date.

Learning to Drive

The prospect of learning-as-you-go can seem pretty daunting. From birth to death we're thrust into a long obstacle course wherein other drivers may or may not know what they're doing, or what we're doing! So, finding a safe way to traverse life isn't easy, especially without solid guidance.

We can forget that we're not the first to face similar dilemmas. History is a handbook that can inspire giant leaps in our spiritual and emotional education. To begin with, our ancestors did not separate the spiritual realm from everyday living. Most people up until about a hundred years ago were intimately aware of their relationship with the Earth, and whatever god they followed. Faith was important; belief and speculation were driving forces.

Today, we seem to have lost the ability to be amazed—to see magic in the spark of a lighter, or in a flight to the Moon. Technology has advanced so far, so quickly, that we shrug off these wonders and talk idly about built-in obsoleteness. In the process, spiritual wonder has gone out of focus in usually one of two extremes. Either people seek after mystical experiences, hoping for the thrilling ride they see in Hollywood's flash and fanfare, or they're too busy to think about other dimensions at all.

For the mystical seekers, they can be pretty disappointed that the route to the divine is sometimes dull. Like most truly worthwhile things in life, learning about the divine and our spirituality takes time, patience, practice, and enough faith to appreciate the process—with or without any miracles. For those "too busy" folks, the spiritual lane is far too uncertain. They stay parked at the curbside of life.

On the highway of life, each of us must begin to identify the difference between personal perceptions, reactions, faith, and reality.

It remains for each of us to find the right motivation —to return to the figurative garage—and start a new learning process, a process that begins in our own hearts. Spirituality is not hocus-pocus. It is not achieved overnight, and possibly not over a lifetime. It is, instead, a way of thinking and being.

Keep It Simple, Be Innovative

Simplicity helps us keep our minds on what's important. Fortitude keeps us going even when life seems like one giant traffic jam. Innovation allows us to meet each of life's detours with humor and personal vision. Put this all together, and you have an excellent foundation for progressive, challenging spirituality that requires nothing more than an open mind, a loving heart, and the willingness to try.

Get Ready to Drive

Fill the Tank

There is absolutely no way someone can drive a car if the gas tank is empty, but a lot of us try to run life when our inner

"spiritual" tanks are empty. In the East, metaphysicians call the universal spirit within each of us "chi" or "ki." When our chi is low, out of balance, or blocked for some reason, sickness and "dis-ease" can result. Consequently, it's very important that we monitor our chi, and make every effort to keep our internal gas tanks filled.

Two easy and effective ways everyone can keep their fuel lines connected to the Divine pump are through regular meditations and prayer. It doesn't matter what facet of the Divine you sit down and talk to, as long as it becomes an integral part of your daily routine. Bear in mind that prayerfulness is as much an attitude as an action, and prayer keeps the lines of energy between you and the your higher self open. Prayer or meditation can become a mini-ritual that focuses our attention back on the limitless potential of the human soul.

It's almost as if everyone needs a personal laptop computer that has http://www.God bookmarked.

Different religious systems treat prayer and meditation from unique perspectives. Some use it to focus energy, while others employ the time to obtain a suitable state of mind for the religious ritual to follow. Others perceive both techniques as a way of drawing the attention of sacred powers, and to cleanse themselves of impurities. Taoists, for example, meditate to expel undesirable ideas and promote inner stillness. Ayurvedic philosophers consider meditation a tool to improve mental hygiene.

Use the Rearview Mirror

Once the inner spiritual tank is topped off, we are ready to face the world; however, there are a lot of other drivers to take into consideration. On the highway of life, each of us must learn to identify the difference between personal perceptions, reactions, faith, and reality. We can do this by looking back.

Our minds automatically default to personal feelings, impressions, and judgments. Consequently, in our quest for the Divine, and our own sense of self, it is very important to find ways to reopen our eyes, readjust perceptions, and get a grip on our core issues.

The Self-Doubt Detour

Many people exaggerate their faults to the point of self-derision. Why is that? What is it about life in the fast lane that causes us to become our own worst critics? At least part of the answer is that our connections to each other are fading through sheer numbers (growing population) and distance (increased mobility). It's hard to feel important and useful when we *mistakenly* feel inconsequential. Many of us tend to overcompensate, driven by the desire to achievement and other superficial images. Consequently, the expectations we place upon ourselves and others can be overwhelming.

> My best advice . . . try and understand how different people communicate about spiritual matters and honor different approaches.

If you find yourself in this scenario, remember that not everyone was born to fame or power, but that doesn't mean we must live in mediocrity either. You are a wholly unique, potential-filled, human being. Making mistakes sometimes, and being brilliant sometimes, is a package deal.

The Perspective Detour

The second roadblock in life is our perspective of others. Everyone has a secret yearning to make his or her life—and everyone in it—conform to an ideal of how things *should be*.

As much as you wish people would respect your spiritual individuality and vision, you also need to show others that respect. Other people can't automatically live up to your expectations—they are not you. Likewise, when friends, family, and coworkers start trying to design your life, don't let their outlooks become your gospel. It's fine to heed good advice, but ultimately you're the primary driver in your life.

Bumpy Road Ahead

Don't automatically accept your cultural, community, or family viewpoint as wholly right. Question everything! You may not always find an answer, or the answer that you wanted, but it's definitely worth the time. Each of these settings represents important traffic circles that we regularly traverse, yet exactly which exit we take from where we are depends on us. Look at what you've been taught, reconsider it in terms of your faith and personal ideals, then merge into the lane most appropriate for you.

A final note: Remember to reward yourself with a well-deserved pat on the back. While many people are quick to admit failure, they're more hesitant to rejoice in success. Pride does not have to equate to egotism and conceit. Instead, allow your pride to act as a powerful substructure that provides confidence in all your endeavors.

Reading Street Signs

Consider how difficult it would be to pass a message to someone who is also driving 65 m.p.h. down a highway—their life path. Personal discourse, particularly on delicate or personal matters, takes on similar hindrances.

The challenges to communication often leads to misunderstandings, misdirected missives, and inaccurate representations between ourselves and others. It's almost as if everyone needs a personal laptop computer that has http://www. God bookmarked.

My best advice is to try and understand how different people communicate about spiritual matters and honor different approaches. For example, many Buddhists feel discussing religious matters is terribly rude, as faith is a private matter for them. Modern fundamentalist Christians, on the other hand, "witness" because the tenants of their faith espouse this as very important for the welfare of others. Neither approach is right or wrong, they are simply different directional signs appropriate to that particular path.

Signal Lights and Horn Blowing

In the fast lane, we have to learn to be active, aware listeners and observers. When we enter into discussions with people, we receive one of the three traffic signals: go, stop, or proceed with caution. This is even more pronounced when talking about religion, sex, and politics.

But, the search for the Divine often requires initiating discussions just to get some fresh outlooks with which to work. Unfortunately, not all these conversations get a green light. In fact, there are times when it seems like you're being called upon to back up and turn around. In this situation, the individual with whom you're trying to communicate has no desire to listen or expose his or her feelings freely.

Center yourself around the steering wheel of your God-self, that still, small voice of higher wisdom within.

Be forewarned that if you choose to run this light, you will get a warning—one that could consist of anything from stern words or harmed relationships to a bloody nose! And don't be surprised if other drivers around you respond by "horning in." Whether or not they agree with you matters little. If you've overstepped, other people are quick about pointing out your error.

Thus, it is important that each of us define, delineate, and respect our own sense of privacy and that of others. Each time we run over someone else's beliefs, it will lead to head-on collisions and other emotional accidents.

This isn't to say that you can't disagree with people. Well-informed, adult debates are healthy. The difference here is in the delivery. Instead of just driving up to someone and tossing your bag of goods unceremoniously at their feet, hand the ideas to them one-by-one, and listen as much as you talk. Everyone will benefit from an exchange when people are open-minded.

Renewing Your License

Assessment periods are highly recommended, and birthdays offer a perfect day to re-evaluate what we know, and provide an opportunity to set ground rules that make sense in our lives here and now. What are your taboos? How do you define good and bad? What is love? What do you want from life? Is your path still challenging and motivating you to be the best human being possible?

These are the questions to ask, and answer, with certainty. Don't get back into the fast lane until you have a heartfelt response. Otherwise, other unscrupulous drivers will be more than happy to define your "right of way" for you.

Balance and continuity have become incredibly important now that we're traveling increasingly crowded roads. It's very easy to have our proverbial apple cart upset by bumps, potholes, or reckless drivers. A life in balance is run by someone who sees the obstacles developing before they become inundating, and then finds proactive ways not only to avoid them, but to do something even better!

A Life in Balance

Center yourself around the steering wheel of your God-self, that still, small voice of higher wisdom within. As you do, it will slowly direct the transformation in your life in ways you never thought possible. Before you know it, you will be cruising the fast lane peacefully with others, with a cool wind at your back, and joyful music in your soul.

Spills & Chills of Ghost Hunting

by Tammy Sullivan

It was like a set from a horror movie.
A small, old graveyard sat on the top of a hill in rural Ohio. Fog had settled over the hill, the Moon was full and bright, and the air was still. I was wandering through the cemetery with my flashlight when a dense patch of smoke caught my attention.

Chills ran up and down my spine as I watched the "smoke" become denser and take shape right in front of me. I screamed and ran to my vehicle. A few moments later, I realized that I had run away from a patch of fog. I was caught up in the moment and I forgot to keep calm and quiet, and to observe—which are the primary objectives for the ghost hunter. Moreover, running through a graveyard at night is risky. It's easy to trip and get hurt.

Why Hunt Ghosts?

Ask any ghost hunter and he or she will give you a myriad of reasons why they hunt ghosts. For me, it is for the possible interaction with another level of existence. The experience is not unknown to me. I've lived in two haunted houses, one of which was very active. Yet I still seek out occasions that may allow me a glimpse into the land of the dead.

Others like to hunt for the excitement. Let's face it, ghosts are exciting. They can appear anywhere at any time and surprise you. A delicious thrill courses through my body when I'm not quite sure what to expect. Still others are searching for a way to prove the existence of ghosts.

Folks seem to want to take all sorts of electronic gadgets—like voice recorders, motion detectors, meters that monitor electrical frequencies, video cameras, and thermometers along with them on their ghost hunts. I prefer to do things the old-fashioned way and make use of magical tools like pendulums, dowsing rods, or the Ouija. However, I do take a flashlight with extra batteries, and I often take my digital camera, a notebook, and pen so I can jot down the time, weather conditions, and any other relevant data concerning possible sightings.

Where Do Ghosts Hang Out?

There are well-known hauntings everywhere from luxury hotels and ships to lighthouses or tiny cabins buried deep in the woods. Graveyards are always a good bet, as are historic areas (especially battlefields). Bridges and crossroads are also prime areas for ghostly activity. Anywhere that's spooky is a good place to start. And it does not have to have a haunted reputation in order to be haunted.

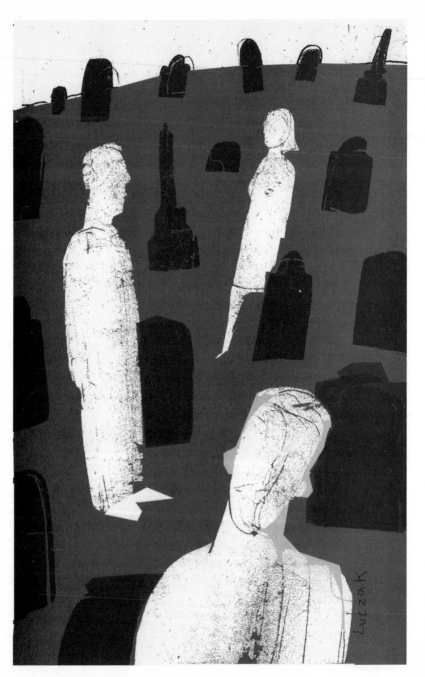

Many people like to say prayers of protection and the like before entering a haunted place, and asking for protection certainly won't hurt anything. When I enter an area, I always introduce myself and state my purpose for being there.

After I settle in, I try to notice any out-of-place things happening, such as my watch stopping (this one is most noticeable when hunting on a bridge), things moving, or faint odors that become stronger before fading away. I've even felt as though I've been touched. But whenever I've felt agitated, irritable, or uncomfortable, I leave the area.

It's very rare to come into contact with a full-body apparition. Shadow creatures are more the norm, but moving shadows aren't always ghosts. They can also be insects, rodents, and any other number of everyday occurrences. The simplest explanation is often the correct one.

Intentions carry weight on the other side of the veil, and if intentions are not positive in nature, it's best to stay home. Ghosts don't seem to mind when we wish to learn, but any attempt to use them for other benefits could be disastrous.

If You Go Ghost Hunting

When ghost hunting, always use commonsense safety rules. No running, screaming, practical jokes, or horseplay. The number one rule when engaging in activity involving spirits is to always be respectful and courteous. Always have a partner for each person and make sure you have permission to be in the area from the property owner. Once the ghost hunt is complete, clean up any litter and take everything back home with you. Don't be surprised if you find that you are very tired and thirsty. It is very common. Just drink plenty of fluids and rest. Don't worry about viewing your pictures or listening to any recordings until after your body is well rested. A cleansing shower with a vinegar splash is also recommended to remove any leftover vibrations.

Also note that antidepressants often block people from experiencing or seeing spiritual activity. If you are taking an antidepressant, be aware that you may not see or feel the signs that a ghost is near, but that does not mean it isn't there.

Happy hunting!

OVER THE CAULDRON

Up-to-date Wiccan & Pagan opinions & rantings overheard & spelled out just for you

WE ARE ALL RIGHT!

by Luna

One Saturday night in early spring, I was sitting by a bonfire, pondering what will happen to me when I die—exactly. I brought out my flute and, staring into the fire, I began to play. I played until I was totally immersed in thinking about my spirituality. Suddenly, I got this feeling of utter and complete weightlessness, and I tell you honestly that I had a feeling of acceptance and genuine understanding for the first time in my life. What follows is the culmination of what I now call my "vision quest."

I played a song on my cedar flute I call "The Whales Tune," because it was the first thing I played while watching humpback whales diving in frigid Alaskan waters a few years ago. The bonfire was high and bright, and intensely hot; yet, the air around me was filled with the chill of early spring.

I was in an ancient woods, walking with bare feet on a thick carpet of leaves and moss. Occasionally, I could hear a cardinal calling—beckoning me to come deeper into the woods. I stepped lightly and quickly as I made my way under a thick canopy and up a small incline. Here the trees opened up in a circle and the sunlight shined brilliantly in the center of the circle, where the greenest grass I've ever seen was growing. There were vivid yellow buttercups peeking up through the grass and pink clover blossoms.

I entered the clearing and lay down on the ground, looking skyward and feeling the earth on the palms of my hands. The warmth from the Sun touched my face and warmed my body. I lifted my hair out from under my neck and nestled into the Mother for a time of quiet solitude. My mind wandered as I heard the cardinal calling from nearby and

I believe in my heart that we are *all* right, and I think the journey I took taught me to appreciate and respect all paths . . .

then he was suddenly further away. I could scarcely hear his call and was straining to hear more when the thought struck me: What if we are *all* right?

I lay in that circle of light, warmed by my thoughts, and went deeper within myself—and deeper into the woods. I wondered if we are *all* right in our beliefs. I wondered if the Divine Light, of which we are all a part, has allowed us to each worship deity in our own way. I wondered if, instead of fighting with one another about semantics over what we each deem is right or wrong in a spiritual path, we could simply respect

one another and learn from each other the various paths open to us. I saw in my mind's eye Muslims, Jews, Protestants, Catholics, Buddhists, Taoists, Pagans, and every other spiritual path, communing. I saw us all acknowledging that which is highest and best in each other and learning acceptance and tolerance. I envisioned people accepting that each path is different in the journey and that the sights along the way are divergent. I was filled with the certainty that each path still leads inexplicably to the same

I have a desire to travel all paths until the warmth from the Sun in that clearing has left my soul.

divinity in the end. I was heartened by the discovery that loving one another, because of the journey, and with open hearts, is the core of my existence.

I continued to lie in the clearing and absorb what is good and true in all of the various paths I noticed opening up around the circle. I heard drums in the forest, I heard chanting in an unknown language, and I heard the call of the animals. I heard many divergent paths opening before me, crossing over one another, merging, becoming one, and uniting toward one great destination.

When I truly opened my heart to all that was surrounding me, I realized then that we are *all* right. Each of us is right in the path that we have chosen for our own spiritual enlightenment. We are all striving toward the end of our own roads, and along the way our paths cross with those of the people in our lives. My path is made smoother by your journey, and by the words and experiences that you share with me. Your path is made smoother by my journey, and by the words and experiences I share with you.

When I realized this fully, when I saw the paths opening up in the circle around me, I stood and called out to the cardinal. I heard his call in the forest ahead of me, not on

the path behind me. I knew then, as I know now, that I cannot travel back through that path. I must follow a different path. I turned around to gaze upon all of the open pathways, and took my first step onto the dark, unknown path ahead of me, knowing in my heart that I would take the warmth of the Sun, and the knowledge you have all shared, into what lay before me.

I realized as I walked onto the unknown path that a coolness approached and surrounded me. An aching had come to my back and legs when I realized I was sitting before very weak embers in what had previously been a raging bonfire. I heard the song lilting from my flute and I felt the ache of my folded legs. I felt the song in my heart and the warmth of the Sun in my heart.

I believe in my heart that we are *all* right, and I think the journey I took has brought me to appreciate and respect all paths. I have a desire to travel all paths until the warmth from the Sun in that clearing has left my soul.

By The Book
by Link

I looked in the yellow pages for a Pagan public school. I didn't find any. Not one. But I did find a variety of metaphysical bookstores and magical supply shops. I went to one of these stores, and there on a book shelf I found all the secrets of the universe. Soft-cover, only $9.99.

So, now I could do magic by the book! I tried calling the four directions, but it took me so long to memorize the exact words. I

tried purifying my sacred space, but I couldn't pronounce all
those ceremonial words. (It was some kinda foreign language;
it sounded like what my Uncle Irving and Aunt Sadie used
to yell when the old station wagon wouldn't start.) I tried
meditating, too; but by the time I got comfortable enough, it
was time to flip the cassette tape over. I would have liked to
have said a simple prayer to the Goddess, but I wasn't to that
chapter in the book yet, so I had to wait.

I went back to the store and the person there said I
wasn't using the right color candle. In fact, I needed not just
one candle, but seventy-two candles! (This is to balance the
numerological energy between my magical name, the phase

of the Moon, the exact weight in grams of my silver jewelry, as well as the last four digits on my Visa card.) And incense. I needed incense. And charcoal. "Don't forget to have extra charcoal," they all warned me.

So when I did my ritual, I lit all seventy-two candles and filled my hibachi full of charcoal. Ninety-one packages (thirteen for each chakra), and incense

And when I think about the Goddess, I call her the Goddess. That's it . . . just the Goddess.

too. I lit the whole pack! Purple Moonbeam Aquarian Sage Ritual Incense. (This is just a code name. I can't find out the real ingredients until after a year and a day.) And oil. I poured in a whole bottle of Peace-Giving Psychic Wisdom Oil. (It's lower in cholesterol than even Canola Oil!)

Whooof!

Well, in a past life, I must've blown out a candle instead of snuffing it—because the fire elementals got real mad. Whooof!!! Between all my candles and all the fumes from my charcoal and incense and oil and stuff, I barely had enough breath to dial 911. The ambulance driver said I had smoke inhalation and was lucky to be alive. (Gee, my first healing spell!)

After all of this, I looked at things a bit differently. I used my books as *one* way to learn from the ideas of others. Many of the authors were very thought-pro-

I stopped worrying about saying all the right words to call the elements or to purify the Circle, and just spoke from my heart instead.

voking, and understanding several different view points helped me form my own opinions. I decided I could learn from the books and still do what felt right for me, and for the moment. While I am very lucky to have freedom of the press,

I realized the greatest book of all is *not* for sale. It is written deep within us all, by a very special Author, and every day we turn a new page. I also found the Old Ways would speak to me through nature, the birds singing, or the thunderstorms, or even that big ol' tree behind the post office.

And now when I shop for the few things I use in rituals, I do it very carefully. I realized some of the people selling me stuff were just that—people selling me stuff! But others were more sincere about their vocation. They seemed more like teachers and mentors rather than Retail Clergy. After a while, it was easy to tell the difference.

I stopped worrying about saying all the right words to call the elements or to purify the Circle, and just spoke from my heart instead. I also discovered that once I stopped trying to use the exact verbatim words, I could actually think about what I was saying, and why it was being said. I like that much better!

I even tried new things, like facing the lake out back, or maybe the ocean, instead of always facing west for water. It just feels right, like politely facing somebody when you speak to them in person. I guess facing west made sense for folks back in England, but where I live water is someplace else! And instead of burning a green candle for earth, I used a little cup of soil from my garden. Any candle—even a green one—is still fire. But there are lots of stuff that, to me, *feel* more like earth.

And when I think about the Goddess, I just call her the Goddess. That's it. No elaborate names I don't fully understand, no historical baggage from all the wars and stuff in the mythology books. Just the Goddess. And when I think about the God, he's just the God. I know they both love me, no matter what phase of the Moon, and even if I'm not dressed in black.

How to Do Magic

I'm not exactly sure how to do magic, but I did find there are plenty of things I do every day, without all the hocus-pocus, that are very magical. Today, I sent my sick friend a get-well card. (Gee, is that a healing spell, too?) And last night, I said a simple thank you before eating dinner. And the night before that, when I took a hot shower, I visualized myself washing away all my tension and stress. Ahhh. Now *that* was magic!

Maybe someday, I'll even write these ideas in my own book. Soft-cover, only $9.99.

What's Your Beef?

by Parthena

When I timidly stepped onto the path
about nine years ago, I walked into a "wom-
en's circle." As I got to know everyone, to
hear their stories and discover their personalities and the group dynamic, I listened
with amusement to the guys complaining
about there being no "men's circle," and
about too much focus on women. When
the women suggested to the men that they
start their own circle, they did; and it died

after only three meetings. File this one under "closed due to lack of interest."

So, guys, what's your beef?

The Truth about "Female" Paganism

At any given time, it seems that a large portion of the books stocked in the New Age section of chain bookstores contain "Goddess" in the title, or mention the Goddess as their main theme. If a male new to Paganism picks up Starhawk's *Truth or Dare* or *Dreaming the Dark* as early reading, he may get the impression that Wicca is a form of feminism.

Sometimes, the fact that a growing number of the books in our genre are written by men isn't all that clear. For example, until I saw his picture on a Web site, I had always thought that Raven Grimassi was female!

Throughout history, Witches have been depicted primarily as female. There's, of course, the Halloween hag and the sexy, mini-skirted Witch at your typical costume party. Laurie Cabot is the celebrity Witch of Salem. And then there's that whole *Charmed* and *Bewitched* thing.

It is widely assumed that during the Burning Times, only women were targeted as Witches. In fact, approximately 20 percent of those accused were male, and none, male or female, were executed for worshipping any Pagan deity.

Despite our best efforts over the past thirty-plus years, we still live in a gender-stereotypical society. Ask any single mother who is raising sons (with a sense of equality), how she feels when the children bring home stereotypical ideas overheard from athletic coaches and teachers. She'll tell you that it often feels like a losing battle.

While we've supposedly achieved equality between the sexes, men are still paid more than women, and they advance further in their careers. Judeo-Christian domination in this country has always maintained that the creator is male,

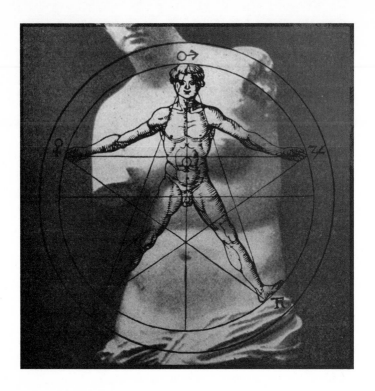

and in some Christian religions, women are still prohibited from serving in a ministerial capacity, or participating in decision making.

In our culture, the so-called "equality" that many women have fought for is basically a sham. Men are still assumed to be stronger and smarter than women, due to a small part of the social sector that refuses to let the myth die.

Males are often socialized by traditions despite the best efforts of their parents, significant others, and their own inner voices. The idea of worshipping a female goddess, or being subservient to an earthly female, is not exactly exciting or easy to accept for most guys in our society.

It's no wonder, then, that men considering the path wonder if Wicca is a female-dominated religion and question whether or not there is a place for them. I think the true question is whether or not it will be a comfortable place for men and women alike.

While the question doesn't seem to rear its head as often as it used to, I still see it brought up quite regularly on online message boards. It's still part of an ongoing discussion that often turns into an argument.

For instance, someone points out that Dianic Witches are the only ones who worship the Goddess exclusively, and then someone else says that Pagans traditionally worshiped the God and Goddess equally until that radical feminist Starhawk came along and ruined everything. Someone then calls Silver RavenWolf an idiot, no one apparently knows the difference between Wicca and Paganism, and we're off to the races on our broomsticks. The person who initially brought up the topic typically leaves shaking his or her head, more confused than ever.

Although feminism reached its peak and struggles under the backlash of anti-feminists, it is not uncommon to encounter a radically feminist teenager.

Anima/Animus

Carl Jung coined the terms "anima" and "animus." Jung maintained that every personality contains aspects of the opposite gender. Anima is the female component, and animus is the male aspect. Jung believed that we need to embrace these aspects and integrate them as part of our personality. The blend of the two energies leads to an emotionally and psychologically healthy person.

Certain symbols in dreams represent these aspects, and the symbols may have different meanings depending on which gender dreamed them. So—end of discussion, right? Actually, not on your life! Whether they've heard of Jung or not, some simply refuse to believe that a mixture of energies is at all necessary in magic or spirituality.

To be fair, there is some basis in the accusation that Paganism is blindly feminist. Books such as Merlin Stone's 1976 work, *When God Was a Woman,* gave a great deal of support to the feminist gripe about patriarchal societies. I became interested in witchcraft in the late 1970s. Living in Santa Monica at the time, I visited a small Wiccan shop to purchase a book I had seen advertised in those little ads in the back of *Cosmopolitan* magazine. The book was *The Feminist Wicca.*

If dedicating yourself to a female deity or being part of a predominantly female group or coven is an issue for you, examine what is at the root of your uncertainty.

I've since lost it in a move and I don't recall who published or wrote it, but I do remember the text. Based on my memory, the book was a sort of Book of Shadows with a lot of basics and some spells. I don't recall anything in the text that was blatantly feminist, although the feminist movement was in all its glory at the time. Still, I didn't choose to take this path until the mid-nineties.

Surprisingly, although feminism reached its peak and struggles under the backlash of antifeminists, it is not uncommon to encounter a radically feminist teenager. Some of these young women come to the path speaking of being thrilled at finding a goddess-based religion, and they balk at the idea of including any male god.

Perhaps they have been homeschooled on patriarchal societies and taught to resist male dominance in any form. While they will mature into strong, assertive women, there is a danger that their hatred of men will seriously detract from relationships, overshadowing positive male traits that, when appreciated, can enhance a relationship. Failure to understand these behaviors on either side can cause serious harm to a relationship. And, of course, these women miss out on the benefits of the notions of balance taught in most Pagan paths.

Feminism brought us to the two-income family and gave men more responsibility for caring for children. Many men have connected with their nurturing side because of feminism and have no qualms today about revealing it in public. Sure, many men still suffer from being encouraged always to "be tough" and to resist revealing their emotions, or any sign of weakness, for fear of being seen as sensitive. And sure, as a result, more men than women over age thirty-five are still dying from heart disease. The fact is, men have made great social strides in the last thirty years, and much of the credit goes to feminism.

Complicated Relations

Wow, life is complicated, isn't it? When we're in sacred space or Circle, we are separated from the mundane. But all good Witches take a bit of sacred back into the mundane, so we can't really separate. Perhaps, one goal should be to improve who we are in the mundane.

If dedicating yourself to a female deity or being part of a predominantly female group or coven is an issue for you, examine what is at the root of your uncertainty. Is it rooted in the mundane, such as an issue that affects your relationship with women? Or is it spiritual, such as having difficulty swallowing the idea that God may be female?

Many goddesses actually incorporate both male and female aspects. The mighty and strong Morrigan is a good example. The Egyptian goddess Sekhmet has been depicted with a phallus in some ancient statues. Athena burst forth from Zeus' head after he swallowed her pregnant mother, and Aphrodite was born from the testicles of Uranus—both were born from a male "womb."

By following these or any number of similar goddesses, you are indirectly honoring the God. Some sabbaths, such as the Winter Solstice, specifically honor the God. In reality, we may be exposed to both energies unintentionally with no escape. A question worth pondering is that while we see gods and goddesses as male and female, do they really even possess any particular gender at all?

Dianic Witches worship one goddess exclusively—Diana. While Dianic covens worship Diana, most recognize the polarity of energies without actually following the God. Wicca and other forms of Paganism are more liberal in this respect.

Although Paganism may be the fastest-growing religion in the world, it is still impossible to obtain accurate statistics as to our numbers or the method of practice. Many individuals still find it necessary to keep their path secret. The best estimate of how many Wiccans and Pagans practice as solitary, rather than in groups or covens, is "most." Practicing as a solitary is necessary for some, since it is dangerous for groups to practice in many parts of the country. If you are practicing as a solitary, then you have complete freedom to choose your method of service to deity—unless you get into an argument on a message board.

Guardians of the Heart

Belonging to a group can have its own set of issues. Elise Coleman and Rick Wilson run Guardians of the Heart in Tulsa, Oklahoma. Elise is a "take charge" kind of woman and very much the high priestess. To the observer, it is obvious that the relationship is an equal partnership free of conflict. Elise is the voice of the group, and Rick works more quietly. When I discussed this with Elise, who practices fairy traditions, she pointed out that Rick practices Asatru, which is a more masculine pantheon.

"However," she says, "Rick is a special kind of guy." Both have achieved the maturity that life experience brings into the relationship and makes it successful.

The group has also achieved a good balance of male and female members since Rick and Elise have been working together. When I asked some of the guys for input on this article, most had nothing to say—no complaints about the amount of female-focus in their group. Musician Lee Spitzer did offer this comment: "Are men being neglected in Wicca? I don't think so. I've seen many men at the circles I've gone to. With a few exceptions, most of the circles I've been to honor *both* the Goddess and God. Personally, I've

> In the end, most groups, even those that are very female centered, at least include a candle dedicated to the God on the altar.

been treated with great respect by everybody in the local Pagan community."

Lee's also a special kind of guy, though. It shows in a song called "Wild Women" on his *Solitary Eclectic* CD. Lee sings of a woman who packs her bags to take a break from the stress of the mundane and be spiritually fed, Pagan style. Lee has followed both a god and goddess and obviously "gets it" when it comes to understanding women.

In the end, most groups, even those that are very female centered, at least include a candle dedicated to the God on the altar. My personal opinion is that if you're going to read *The Charge of the Goddess* you should read *The Charge of the God*, as well.

If you choose to follow the God as well as the Goddess and feel that he is being slighted, talk to the high priest or priestess. Anything can become stagnant over time, and they may not realize this could be true of their ritual. I've belonged to groups where the leader was on an ego trip and members were afraid to speak up. If that's the case, it has very little to do with deity—it's a personality disorder. You may want to seriously consider finding another group.

If you just feel out of place with a group that is predominately female, get over it. If it's a healthy group, male membership will grow in time. Unless you choose to practice a particular pantheon, deity is a matter of personal and spiritual preference.

Many Wiccans and Pagans, including myself, say that it took them a few years to identify with any god or goddess at all. Our patrons can, and in my opinion should, change as we change. I also believe that the gods and goddesses claim us when we need them. Learn to listen.

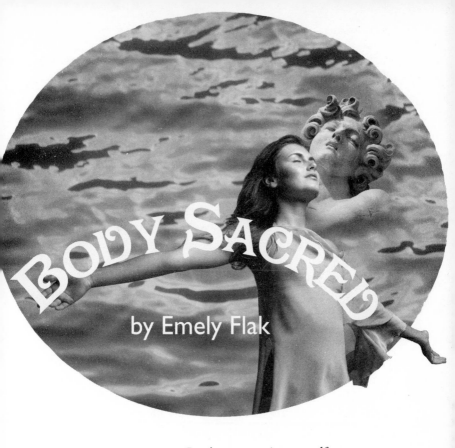

BODY SACRED

by Emely Flak

*Don't compromise yourself; you
are all you've got.* —Janis Joplin

Regardless of your age or body shape,
your body is sensual, unique, and represents the many forms of the Goddess.
Along with nurturing your mind and soul,
your optimal well-being also relies on you
honoring your body. Too often, we neglect
our body or deny it the true love and celebration it deserves. Celebrating our bodies helps us connect to our goddess energies and acknowledge the gift of feminine

essence within. It's recognizing the triple goddess—maiden, mother, and crone—as she manifests in each woman. When you lavish your body with self-love, sexuality, and confidence, along with sensible nutrition and exercise, you give yourself permission to shine!

Self-Love

The first love spell you ever cast should be for yourself. A ritual honoring your body will help you heal any past pain and help you accept that your body is designed to give and receive pleasure. You have heard some people refer to their bodies as their "temple." This is not as silly as it sounds. This approach helps you to consider yourself a sex goddess.

Invoke your inner goddess and celebrate your body with a ritual on a Friday night. Friday is the day that corresponds to Venus, Roman Goddess of love and beauty. Light a pink candle and take a long bath with your favorite oils. Pink represents love, self-love, and acceptance. After you have luxuriated in your bath, dry yourself slowly. In the candlelight, massage your body with lotion or oil as you imagine yourself being prepared as a goddess in a temple. Look in a mirror (full length, if possible) and say:

Venus, Aphrodite, I invoke thee
With your acceptance and love bathe me.
My body is a gift and shrine of pleasure
Like all women in time I am a goddess treasure.

After your bath ritual, feel the warmth and love spread through your body. Dedicate your thoughts to goddesses of love, to awaken the spirit of Aphrodite or Venus by saying:

I honor my body. It brings me pleasure and brings pleasure to others.

Unleash Your Body Confidence

The way you carry yourself—your body confidence—is a powerful aphrodisiac. You don't have to look like a cover girl or have the figure of a supermodel to exude sex appeal. Being comfortable with *who you are* is as important as being proud of your body. Self-love is not selfish or indulgent; it's a necessary tool to help you connect with your feminine divine. With this confidence and comfort, you are better equipped to share your warmth with others. To promote body confidence, indulge in a physical activity that allows you to express your sensuality. You could belly dance to your favorite exotic music to feel sexy and feminine. Experiment with ways to move your body sensually and with pride.

Sexuality

Your body is designed to give and receive exquisite pleasure; something that should never make you guilty or ashamed. When you experience the most exquisite physical pleasure of sexual union, you will recognize it as a divine gift from the Goddess. Sex is a sacred exchange of physical energy and an incredibly potent way to raise magical energy. Sexuality can be experienced through various ways. It can be for love, passion, or pure lust; it can be experienced with spontaneity and romance, or with yourself.

Moon Blessing

In Western culture, for too long, our monthly bleeding has been viewed with negativity or as something to disguise. Welcome your moonflow as an integral connection to goddess energy. Just as you work magic with the lunar cycles by aligning your intent and actions with the waxing and waning of the Moon, become attuned to your natural energy and emotional fluctuations that are linked to your menstrual cycle. Welcome your moonflow as a blessing, not a curse. Enjoy and celebrate this aspect of your feminine essence that affirms the sacred connection between your feminine energy and the lunar cycles.

In some cultures, the menstrual blood is regarded a sacred fluid. While menstruating, most women are more intuitive, making it an optimal time for psychic work. In some cultures, when women live in close proximity, they bleed near the same time. Among the Native American tribes, it was common for women to separate themselves from the rest of the tribe for a period of rest and contemplation while they were "mooning." Synchronized periods can also occur where women share a working or domestic environment.

Try this affirmation to celebrate your body at your moonflow time:

> *My body is blessed by the Moon and I celebrate the flow of my feminine essence.*

Croning

When a woman can no longer give birth, when her monthly blood flow has ceased, she is in the crone phase—long associated with suppression and dread—of the female cycle. In tribal societies, the older women, or crones, were revered as "wise women"— the keeper of women's mysteries and unparalleled wisdom. Sadly, in developed countries, most women today approach menopause with dread, fear, and even denial.

Instead of fighting this natural rhythm, you can choose to accept it with ritual and ceremony. Share the experience with a group of supportive, like-minded friends. Be proud of the inner guidance your wisdom and maturity will reward you with. As a time that is associated with freedom from maternal responsibilities, it is a powerful time for women. If you are croning and experience discomfort with the physical changes, seek advice from a natural therapist who will recommend herbal supplements that will be kinder to your body.

Daily Self-Care

Along with ritual and celebration, remember the importance of a balanced diet, regular exercise, drinking ample water, adequate sleep and rest, and slow, deep breathing. The key to quality physical care is balance: you can enjoy that glass of wine and piece of decadent chocolate cake without guilt if you maintain a healthy perspective on moderation.

Honoring your body is a way to connect to your goddess energy. With celebration, ritual, and visualization, you treat your body with the love and care it deserves. To receive the best, you first need to believe that you are entitled to happiness and pleasure. When a woman accepts her true self, and celebrates her own inner and outer beauty, she becomes the irresistible woman that she was always meant to be. Celebrate and enjoy the goddess within you!

BELIEVE AND ACHIEVE

by Link

Psychic power. We use it every day.
We cause things to happen; we shape events with our minds. We can do this, because every thought is a prayer.

Thoughts are a powerful form of energy. They are very real and very potent. Look for their energy not just in deep meditation or altered states of mind, but any time! In fact, your life is more likely to be shaped by what goes through your mind during your daily shower than during meditation.

When we first discover magic and spirituality, we tend to clearly define when we are "doing it" and when we are not. We draw nice little lines that clearly separate religion from the rest of our thoughts and deeds. "Now I'm in Circle" or "Now I'm working magic." Over time, we begin to erase those lines as we discover that we are always in Circle, we are always working magic! Erasing the dividers between religion and the rest of your life makes even simple events special—and very powerful.

If you believe in the power of positive thinking, you know that thoughts and words have real significance. Phrases like "with my luck" usually tend to focus on how we might fail. They actually add energy to the failure side of the equation. Sometimes we even begin planning what we'll do after this failure occurs, which allows the possibility of failure to become more real.

If you believe in the power of positive thinking, you know that thoughts and words have real significance.

A very basic magical technique involves discussing what you want as if it has already happened. For example, you think about what you will do now that you already have a new job, good health, and a happy mate. Believing as if what you want *is already so* adds energy to the side of the equation that brings you success.

Remember that other people's thoughts are just as real as your own. When you hope for the best, tell someone who will sincerely *believe* along with you. This person becomes a sort of magical partner, adding their own energy to your wish. Your magical wishes are like great big balloons, filled with energy from your thoughts and deeds. Someone supportive helps fill your magical balloons by adding not just energy, but very tangible aid (wise advice, experience, networking contacts, or other tools they might offer) to help you succeed.

Often, magic occurs through truly ordinary actions. But choose wisely in whom you confide. Your loving family might truly want to see you succeed, but would your jealous coworkers? This is one valid basis for magical secrecy. Try to be aware of how others might poke leaky energy holes in your magic.

Do you believe in visualization? Is the apple in your mind as real as the apple in your fruit basket? If you can conceive it, and believe it, then you truly can achieve it! Visualization isn't limited to some complex yoga-style ritual. It can be as simple as making an analogy in conversation, because an analogy helps people make connections with your words. Visualization can also be a simple daydream before you climb out of bed. In fact, what we do during that crucial snooze-alarm period may set the tone for the rest of the day.

Be Careful What You Visualize

If every thought is a prayer, imagine what happens when you spend time thinking about crime and war and hate and violence. Now multiply your thoughts times millions of people, all of whom are visualizing the same thing at the same time. Sound powerful? Well, I've just described what happens each day when America watches the six o'clock news! Mass media helps millions to all visualize a common image. And what does TV news tend to dwell on? The sad aspects of life. (Perhaps in some cases, ignorance truly is bliss.)

We often say that divinity resides within. If so, then when we talk to ourselves, we talk to the Divine. Living your everyday life is like having a constant conversation with the Goddess and God. Within your own mind, within your own heart, every thought is a prayer.

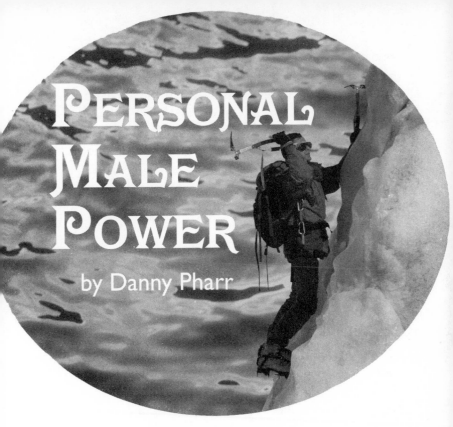

PERSONAL
MALE
POWER

by Danny Pharr

Masculine power is an elusive trait for many men. The worship of the Goddess and the many forms of matriarchal spirituality have in some ways neutered the male Pagan persona. The problem is not that men are not masculine or that women are not feminine. The problem is one of balance.

In every man and in every woman there are both the masculine and feminine aspects of the human experience. The key to stepping fully into individual power is, first, to fully embody the aspect to which you are most drawn. This means for most men the masculine and for most women the feminine. Also, one needs to create a sense of masculine-feminine balance through relationships.

Men and Women Out of Balance

The key dynamic that brings men and women out of balance and into a state of victimhood is mistrust. When a woman doesn't trust that the masculine energies will be held by the man, then she devotes some of her feminine energies to masculine ends, which steals the male's power and reduces hers. And, in doing so, she develops a tiny distrust in the male's ability to embody the masculine power.

This distrust grows in strength every time you are tested and fail, thereby creating the need for further testing (generally, this occurs subconsciously). Once you can claim your personal masculine power, you will create a safe balanced space for you and for your partner. Similarly, you will also reshape your relationships with men, although this will occur through respect and admiration.

The masculine seeks freedom, emptiness, victory, success, and triumph over adversity. The feminine seeks fullness, wholeness, praise, and community; and both bond and grow through the attainment of their respective goals.

Claiming Masculine Power

Claiming personal masculine power is like attaining any other goal; there are specific skills involved and action is required. Masculine power comes from knowing what you want, standing firm in your convictions, and changing your course and your mind when the situation warrants such changes.

A single metaphor for achieving success, coupled with five power tools and five power boosters, will generate tremendous amounts of personal power. The great thing about this

metaphor, these power tools, and these power boosters, is that you are already adept in their use.

Make the Effort

Little in life is gained without making an effort. Whether your goals are large or small, professional or personal, financial or emotional, your goals will only be achieved by rallying your resources, and applying those resources to the direct attainment of your goals.

Claiming personal power, or reclaiming the masculine in your life, is a worthy goal, and a mandatory goal for anyone who expects to achieve any sort of balance or success. So don't let yourself be guided by fear of failure.

This world is full of metaphor, and metaphor is the way meaning is often assigned to actions and occurrences. You might stand on a mountaintop feeling the power of the wind that gusts, swirls, and pushes, or you might notice a single condor floating on the wind currents in the canyon below. In either case, you might think of yourself and how your life is similar to the wind or the condor.

Three Steps to Success

Get Out of Bed

Get out of bed can mean "take the first step," "prepare for the journey," or "become aware of reality, the surroundings, and facts."

In this case, "get out of bed" means all three. Before anything can be accomplished, preparations must be made. You have to prepare yourself mentally, emotionally, financially, spiritually, and physically.

Mentally, you must be prepared to change, be confident in your ability, believe in yourself, and visualize your future.

Emotionally, you must be prepared to change, be grounded in the present, learn to manage fear and create happiness for yourself.

Financially, you must be prepared to change, be willing to change your lifestyle for the better, willing to change your relationship to money, and willing to act on what's most important.

Spiritually, you must be prepared to change, to take an active role in your spiritual life, and to act on every prayer.

Physically, you must be prepared to change, to eat well, be healthy, and sleep regularly.

All of these changes will create in you a great source of personal power.

Decide What to Do

Nothing happens until you decide that it will happen. Making a decision about your future is so incredibly important that it must be made immediately. Yet, for the same reason, many people put off deciding what to do with their lives because they are afraid of making the wrong choice. In life, any choice causes movement, and the only wrong choice is the one made by not choosing. As long as you follow your heart, your choice will never be wrong.

Deciding what to do with your life can be a joyous experience, or it can be fraught with fear. The joy comes from pursuing your passion. Regardless of what that passion might be, by chasing it, by living it, by embodying your passion you are creating joy. Fear comes from the "What if . . . ?" questions that you end up asking yourself, answering, and then allowing to decide your fate for you.

"What if I don't make enough money?" "What if my family disapproves?" And on, and on, it goes.

The one fact that is often forgotten in the asking and answering of the "What if . . . ?" questions is that such questions are based in only one possible future, a future that would be created only by not deciding to follow your passion, allowing your decisions to be made for you by someone else, and giving up on yourself.

Do It

After a decision is made, the next step is to take action, massive action. Immediate action is required if you are to stay committed to your decision. Deciding to do something creates a huge amount of energy. To make use of this energy, this power, you must take immediate and massive action toward bringing that decision to fruition. This requires formulating a quick vision that represents the new goal that came from that decision, a vision that you can use as a guidepost to show you the way.

Demonstrate your firm commitment to that decision and resulting goal by taking immediate and massive action. Demonstrate your commitment to yourself and your choice by telling other people about your decision, your goal, and what you will do.

Do not just tell them, or yourself, what you intend to do. Rather, commit to what you will do, and do it.

Once you have taken the first step and are firmly committed to the goal that came from your decision, providence will get behind you and will help with each step. The more action you take the more help you will get; conversely, the less action you take, the less help you get.

Decisiveness and massive action have a symbiotic relationship. Decisiveness is useless without some kind of action, and taking massive action is ridiculous unless you are following a conscious choice.

The five steps for claiming your power, or achieving any goal, are: choosing the goal, making a commitment to that goal, focusing on the goal, acting to achieve the goal, and having faith that the goal is worth achieving.

Five Power Tools

The five power tools—decisiveness, commitment, focus, action, and faith—will become a great source of personal power when used and practiced daily. The most successful people in the world today, and throughout history, have utilized these tools to their maximum.

Decisiveness

Decisiveness must come before all else. We can do nothing without first deciding to do so. Decisiveness means change, and change can be a very fearful experience.

When we examine the fear that is felt around making a change, we find that the change itself is not what is feared, but the possible implications of that change. Nothing is certain until it occurs, and the fear of change is based in being uncomfortable with a future that is not certain.

Decisiveness is fearlessness. When you make a decision, you send a very important message to your psyche. You avow that you are courageous, fearless, and most of all committed to your course. You also send a message to other people that you are powerfully decisive.

Commitment

Commitment is your personal declaration of what will be. Commitment is nothing more than your decision, reaffirmed regularly, and acted upon consistently. Commitment is the application of yourself to the pursuit of your dreams.

Commitment is also about setting boundaries in your life, boundaries that serve to direct your energy, your actions, and your beliefs. You delineate what actions are fruitful and what actions are wasteful and off the track when you commit to your course.

Commitment is also accepting the possibility of all conceivable outcomes, even while you are expecting only the outcome desired. Fear is an illusion, and, as Vince Lombardi said, faith is contagious. The present is the only reality, and action helps eliminate fear.

. . . the five power boosters— paying attention, speaking the truth, asking for what you want, taking responsibility, and keeping your agreements —will enhance the speed at which you attain success . . .

Focus

Focus is the ability to block out all stimuli that are not aligned with the intent and purpose of your commitment. The phenomenon of losing track of time when fully focused is thought in some spiritualities to be a period when the consciousness is in direct contact with the Divine. This is called by scholars "liminal space," a concept that describes the moment when humans experience greatest joy.

When you're completely focused on a project, a particular part of the brain takes over and other parts of the mind are temporarily freed of responsibility. The mind relaxes, forgetting about time and place, and acquires the feeling of divine connection, which is simply happiness. Freed from worries, fears, and future possibilities, and truly living in the moment, we are happiest.

Focus is concentration and conceptualization. By focusing on your goals, you allow your mind to fully engage in the process. When you bring all your resources into play, you are better able to realize success because you are focused on success.

"God helps those who help themselves" is a common saying, and it is true.

By focusing on the task at hand, and on your long-term goals, you send a message that you are powerful; that you let nothing stand in your way and no one dissuade you from your course. You know in your heart that your course is the right one for you.

Action

Action is movement of the psyche, movement of the mind, and movement of the body. Action is a message. When you act to fulfill your dreams, you send a message of commitment to everyone, including yourself. You're showing that your dreams and goals are important, attainable, and that they are becoming reality.

This is a powerful message. Action is progress. To get anywhere, to achieve anything, you have to move in that direction, and you have to act to achieve. Success only occurs after you take action toward attaining your desires.

Action is the journey and success is the destination. Action is where personal growth occurs and where joy is found. Wisdom is gained when you face challenges and fears.

To learn and grow, you must experience, and to experience you must act. Action is life. When people talk about experiencing life, they are often talking about action, about the activities they engage in, about their experiences and the journey.

Faith

Faith is the unmitigated belief in something you can't see or prove. Faith is action; faith is a verb. Faith has value only when it's used. Faith comes before, and is a very important aspect of, personal power and success. In order to succeed, you must have faith that the goal you seek is worth attaining. You must have faith that you are worthy of success. You must have faith that you can achieve any goal you set.

Faith is trust. Faith does not mean waiting for someone, be it a person or the Goddess, to do something for you. Having faith means trusting in the process and working toward your goals. It is believing that if you work toward your goals you will receive all the help you need.

"God helps those who help themselves" is a common saying, and it is true. Likewise, so do people help those who help themselves. If a friend asked you for help with a move, you would surely agree. However, if you had done all the work while your friend sat on the couch and watched television, you would very likely have stopped helping.

We only like to help people who help themselves. And, we only receive help when we act for ourselves. Faith is power. The more faith we have in ourselves, the more powerful we feel.

The Five Power Boosters

Power boosters are additional tools you can use to accelerate your success. When you do these five things—pay attention, speak your truth, ask for what you want, take responsibility, and keep your agreements—you will greatly enhance both the speed at which you attain success and the quality of your successes.

Generally, people are glad to give you anything you ask for, especially when you ask with sincerity and respect.

The power boosters, in conjunction with the power tools, are an unstoppable combination. When you use them together, you will claim your personal power.

Pay Attention

Paying attention will dramatically enhance your personal power. When you pay attention to someone or something, you live your life to its fullest because you fully participate. When you pay attention, you receive all of the information available in any situation, and you show respect for yourself and the people around you.

When you attentively focus on another person—listen to their words, watch their movements, and make them feel comfortable and safe—you give that person the wonderful gift of your time and interest. And by giving this gift, you also gain personal power.

Speak Your Truth

Speaking your truth is a source of safety and power in any situation. Truth cannot be wholly understood, for it is far too big.

However, the truth from an individual perspective is available to each of us. Truth is the one thing that everybody believes in, but the nature of truth is seldom grasped. The truth is touted by all of us as fact, and yet the truth, like beauty, is in the eyes of the beholder. We all know when we hear the truth and when we hear something that is not true. The truth simply sounds different.

Whether we call it salesmanship, charisma, entertainment, or good story telling, not telling the truth has a negative affect on self-image. Not speaking the truth will steal personal power, but speaking the truth in all circumstances will greatly enhance personal power.

Ask for What You Want

When you ask for what you want, you are open to cooperation and assistance in any situation. There is tremendous power in asking for what you want. Generally, people are glad to give you anything you ask for, especially when you ask with sincerity and respect. There is a saying among firewalk instructors: "Serve me by allowing me to serve you." When you ask for what you want with sincerity and respect, people have an opportunity to feel good about themselves and to give you help.

The key to getting what you want from others, and from yourself, is to ask for what you want. If you do not state your desires, if you do not record them for your own reference, if you do not acknowledge that you have desires, you will never fulfill them.

You must ask for what you want from yourself in a manner that will wake up both your conscious and unconscious self. This will involve making a record of your desires, a system of accountability, a review process, and visualizing your future. By asking for what you want, you are telling yourself and everyone around you that you are worthy, and powerful enough to attain them.

Take Responsibility

Taking responsibility will dramatically enhance your personal power, and provide you with the ability to change any situation. When you allow a situation, circumstance, or individual to change your mood you are giving your power away. If you feel victimized when something makes you late, or someone cuts you off in traffic, lies to you, takes a parking place, cheats you, or gossips about you, you are becoming a victim. You are allowing something or someone to dictate your emotional state.

We experience the world through our emotions. When we allow our emotional state to be decided by something or someone outside of ourselves, we allow others to decide our experience of the world for us. Taking responsibility does not mean accepting the blame, but it does mean we have to make a choice. We must choose how we feel, how we react, and how we will experience the world.

Destiny is a choice. We shape our destinies by the choices we make every minute of every day.

Choice is power, and the power of choice leads you to success. When you truly own your experience you will claim your personal power.

Keeping Your Agreements

Keeping your agreements will dramatically enhance your personal power. Your reliability in any situation is apparent when you keep your agreements. It exhibits respect for yourself and for the people around you. When you do not follow through on your agreement, others feel disrespected, and at some level deep inside, you disrespect yourself.

By keeping your agreements you show others that you are respectful, and that you are reliable and responsible. By keeping your agreements you show others that you are worthy of their trust and their time, and that you are worthy of their commitments. By keeping your agreements you show others you are capable, honorable, and credible. By keeping your agreements, you model the behavior you expect from others. By showing respect, you will be respected. By trusting, you will be trusted. By honoring, you will be honored. By keeping your agreements, you will be asking others to do the same.

In the same way that keeping your agreements models behavior that you expect from others, keeping your agreements also sends a message to the self. By holding yourself to a higher standard of behavior, you show yourself that you are reliable, responsible, capable, honorable, and credible. By holding yourself to a higher standard of behavior, you validate and enhance your self-reliance, self-respect, self-responsibility, self-trust. Keeping your agreements is an amazing source of personal power.

Martyrdom and Destiny

Martyrdom is the act of turning on yourself for the benefit of another. There is never a circumstance that martyrdom is both expected and appreciated. Even if there were, martyrdom does not serve you, or the greater good. Only by serving yourself, by acting in your own best interest and owning your choice, can you truly claim your masculine power.

Destiny is a choice. We shape our destinies by the choices we make every minute of every day. You can choose to follow your dreams and create the life that you want. Please do not settle for less. Life should feel joyful.

Claiming Your Masculine Power

Personal power is elusive and must be guarded at every moment. Anytime you lose focus and do not pay attention, anytime you do not speak the truth, anytime you accept what you are given without asking for what you want, anytime you do not take responsibility for your experience, and anytime you do not keep your agreement—you lose self-respect and respect from others; you lose trust in yourself and experience a loss of trust from others. You give away your personal power.

Claim your personal masculine power and keep hold of it. Believe in yourself. The three steps for success and the five power boosters are available to each of us at all times. The only reason we would not use them is if we chose not to do so. Personal power is yours for the taking. Claim your power and experience your joy.

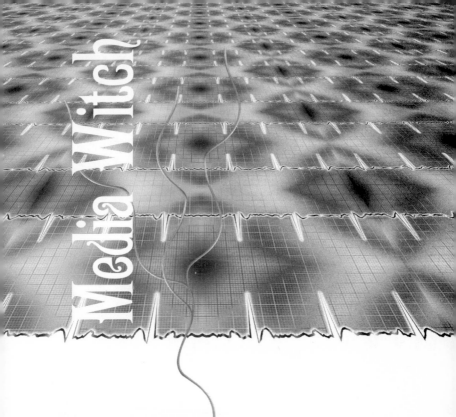

Media Witch

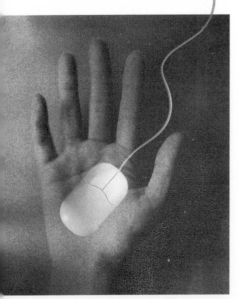

The Witchy Wide
Web, technology, &
electronic magic

Blog the Gods

by Jason Pitzl-Waters

If you pay attention to news stories about the Internet, you'll notice a recent explosion of coverage for "God Bloggers." These are religious men and women who have embraced the latest technologies of the Internet, and they use the technology to spread their personal message(s) of faith. Blogging, once the sole purview of a few enthusiasts, has now exploded in popularity to the point where clergy, theologians, and religious news sites have claimed and benefited from this relatively new technology. Thanks to the ease of use and the ubiquity of the Internet in most American homes, libraries, and cafes, almost anyone can now electronically publish their thoughts, rants, and musings on any subject, religious or otherwise. It was only a matter of time before modern Pagans (a tech-savvy group, if there ever was one) recognized a good thing and joined in. If you haven't already jumped into this fascinating world of expression and amateur journalism, consider this an invitation to explore the world of Pagan blogging.

So, What's A Blog?

A "blog" (short for web log) is, simply speaking, an online journal. Free or for-fee Internet tools abound that allow for easy placement of regular updates onto a personalized Web site. Blog technology has been embraced by people everywhere. From big corporations like Microsoft to open-source Linux enthusiasts, from dyed-in-the-wool conservatives to proud bleeding-heart liberals, from retired folk to businesswomen and home-based moms, from the serious to the lighthearted, blogging is a truly a universal tool.

One of the reasons for the rampant popularity of blogging is that it not only provides you a soapbox, or a stage, but it provides you tools that allow your readers to talk back to you, creating communities where before there were only lone voices. Some of these online communities have become immense through blog media. They have altered public opinion, broken scandals, created surprise bestsellers, and redefined traditional modes of fact-finding and journalism. In short, the blog may be one of the most powerful—some would say magical—tools for change you'll ever handle.

My own introduction to blogging came years ago, when the "blogosphere" was still a rather small village. Talk of how blogs would change things was just that—talk. When I started my very first Pagan-themed blog I was practically alone out there. Most modern Pagans and Witches seemed to prefer more communal and often anonymous communication services, like messageboards and chatrooms. Others built Web pages that served the opposite purpose: static, infrequently-updated personal vanity pages, where visitors were seen (counted) but not heard. Even today you can do an informational search for Pagans on the Internet and find hundreds of abandoned Wiccan Web sites, a similar smattering of half-finished electronic Books of Shadows on each one.

The real revolution regarding Pagans and blogging began in 1997, with the launch of what would become the most popular Web site for Wiccans, Witches, and modern Pagans. In that year, two Witches left the witchcraft advocacy organization WLPA (Witches' League for Public Awareness) to start their own Web site dedicated to fostering communication and unity within the witchcraft (and later, Pagan and Heathen) community. Their Web site became The Witches' Voice (www.witchvox.com). This site was radically different from most sites dedicated to Paganism in that it featured regularly updated content and essays, and the first widely read Pagan blog, "Wren's Nest Spirit News," by cofounder Wren Walker.

While Wren's Nest never identified itself as one, it carries many of the identifying features of a blog. It is updated regularly (daily, in fact); it is organized chronologically, with individual posts one can link to, and it allows readers to comment on each post. While Wren rarely opines on the news links and essays she shares with her readership (aside from the occasional "Chirp"), this site proved that blogging is something that could work for Pagans as a mass audience. In the years that followed, many other bloggers have been inspired

by (or have simply imitated) Wren's approach. This paved the way for the blogging community we have now.

Wren's Nest and Witch's Voice notwithstanding, for many Pagans, blogging was still too complicated for the novice user. One had to learn how to use HTML Internet coding in order to update Web sites manually. But in 1999, two online services were launched that would simplify the process of starting your own blog. Blogger.com and LiveJournal.com each provide simple questionnaire formats for entering personal information and design preferences, and their basic service levels enable any Pagan to start their own blog for free. Now, just about anyone can have a blog of their own. All you need is Internet access and a desire to share your thoughts with the rest of the world. To judge by the hundreds of Pagan blogs currently active, and the millions of blogs of all sorts, it appears that many people do have this desire.

Modern Pagans and heathens, of various dispositions and from all walks of life, have emerged to put the plural to the term "God Blogging"—God Bloggers.

Blogging Into the Future

What follows here is my own (somewhat biased) list of quality blogs by modern Pagans. These Web logs exemplify the potential of Pagan Blogging, and indicate where the future of religion blogging and the Pagan community may be heading.

"Letter From Hardscrabble Creek"

A Pagan writer's blog by Chas S. Clifton
http://www.chasclifton.com/blogger.html

Pagan professor and author Chas Clifton (author of *Her Hidden Children: The Rise of Wicca and Paganism in America* and editor of the Witchcraft Today Series for Llewellyn) has been maintaining this thoughtful and insightful blog since 2003. While this excellent writer doesn't update his blog as often as

I would wish, his posts offer a unique view of our religious history and how it relates to what happens today. From practical nature religion to the legal role of entheogens (peyote, for example), Clifton leads the pack of professional authors who have carried their authorial expertise into the rapidly-expanding blogosphere.

"Peacock Dreams and Other Things"
Musings by T. Thorn Coyle
http://www.thorncoyle.com/musings.htm

Feri priestess, teacher, and author of *Evolutionary Witchcraft*, T. Thorn Coyle shares an eclectic mix of commentaries and spiritual insights on her regularly updated journal. Politics, travel, sex, spiritual practice, and communing with the Divine are all extensively covered. I found Thorn's blog essential reading, alternately inspiring and thought-provoking, when I was doing some spiritual soul-searching not too long ago. Her writing really resonates with the compassionate commitment that exists in our communities, to make the world a better place. Thorn's blog is an essential stop for anyone interested in where our future may (or should) go.

"MacRaven"
Dave Haxton's Weblog
http://www.haxton.org/weblog

Dave Haxton is something of a modern-day Renaissance man. This former software engineer runs his own organic farm in Indiana, is part of an Internet radio station dedicated to Northern European folk music, and maintains a blog detailing his faith, politics, and whatever else happens to cross his path. This is one of the best Asatru (Norse Paganism) blogs out there. Haxton provides a candid look into matters of internal politics, and important matters relating to his faith tradition. A much-needed voice from a often-misunderstood religion.

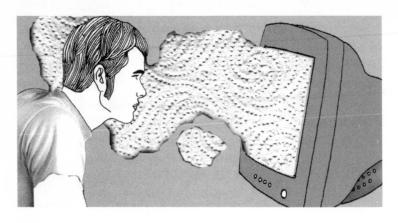

"Roots Down"
A blog by Deborah Oak
http://branchesup.blogspot.com

Psychotherapist, artist, Witch, and activist Deborah "Oak" Cooper maintains a highly thoughtful and personal blog. If you ever wanted to get an inside look at how modern Paganism is lived on a day-to-day basis, this blog is an essential resource. Oak shows how the seemingly ordinary can become sacred, and vice-versa. Love, gardening, popular fiction, activism, and relating to friends are all topics that get covered here, in a voice that stands out from others for its maturity and wisdom.

"Driving Audhumla"
A blog by Victoria Slind-Flor
http://vsf.blogs.com/driving_audhumla

If Deborah Oak's blog catalogues the "inner" workings, then journalist Victoria Slind-Flor's blog is all about the "outer." Peppered with photos from her extensive travelling, along with colorful commentary on public festivals, crafts, conventions, and intimate get-togethers, Oak's blog is all made possible by her silver car "Audhumla" that "gets her where she wants to go," according to her online biography. This is the

Pagan life led outdoors, among fellow Pagans; a beautifully affirming site, and a breath of fresh air.

"Property of a Lady"

A blog by Deborah Lipp
http://www.deborahlipp.com/wordpress

Deborah Lipp, author of *The Way of Four: Create Elemental Balance in Your Life,* has a blog that seems to truly be an extension of her personality. Lipp goes on about Wicca, politics, James Bond, Paganism, and kittens—not necessarily in that order. Her entries about cats and James Bond mix with political rants and reports about the Pagan community in Brazil (and everywhere else). Conversational and responsive, Lipp's blog is an inviting place to visit on the Internet.

"The Wild Hunt"

A modern Pagan perspective by Jason Pitzl-Waters
http://www.wildhunt.org/blog.html

Of course I couldn't finish this section without a bit of shameless self-promotion. This is my own blog, updated daily and focusing on the cultural and political struggles of modern Pagans and their allies. Often sarcastic, but usually relevant, my blog has strived to act as a newsmagazine for Pagans and members of other minority religions. In addition to my daily look at the news, my blog features longer pieces on the role of religion in politics, a weekly feature highlighting modern Pagan musicians, and an occasional post highlighting other Pagan blogs. Not a bad place to visit, even if I do say so myself.

More Favorites

Due to space limitations I couldn't list all of my favorite blogs, but I will quickly give some last shout-outs to:

"At the End of Desire"
http://attheendofdesire.blogspot.com

"Goddessing" http://www.goddessmystic.com

"Quaker Pagan Reflections"
http://quakerpagan.blogspot.com

"Blog o' Gnosis" http://www.gnosiscafe.com/gcblog

"Views From The Cyberhenge"
http://www.neopagan.net/blog

As with all things on the Internet, change is a constant. Don't be surprised if an Internet address doesn't work—nothing is 100 percent certain!

If You Want to Be a Blogger

I'm hoping that this article has inspired you, not only to go out and read Pagan blogs, but perhaps to start your own blog. While the Pagan blogoshpere has grown by leaps and bounds, it only becomes richer as more people participate in it. A bigger Pagan community means that more issues are reported, more theology is discussed, and more interaction happens.

There are several services out there that make it very easy to start your own blog. You can simply head to Blogger. com or LiveJournal.com and follow the directions to open an account. If you prefer more flexibility and control, you can research one of the more robust services being offered. A simple Google search will present you with a host

While you don't have to update every day . . . once a week is suggested if you are going to become a regular resource for other Pagans.

of options (many of them cost-free). Leaving technical considerations aside, I would like to give some tips on good Pagan blogging.

Pick Your Topic(s)

What will you write about? Is there a certain topic that interests you? Is there something you feel hasn't been covered adequately already? If you plan to write online regularly, play to your strengths. What do you know a lot about; what do you have to offer; what is your particular perspective?

In for the Long Haul?

Once you have an idea about the topics and subject matter you would like to focus on, the next thing is to consider if you are ready to write on a regular basis (regular, of course, to be defined by you). Lots of blogs get started with high hopes, only to stop after a couple weeks. Make sure you have the fire and commitment necessary to keep your blog going. If you think you might get sick of your blog after a couple of months, you might want to reconsider.

Update Regularly

This is an important one. If you can't update on a regular basis—weekly, monthly, or seasonally—then no one will read your blog except yourself (and maybe some loyal friends). Blogs live and die by their updates. While you don't have to update every day, at least once a week is suggested if you are going to become a regular resource for other Pagans.

Link, Link, Link!

Link to other blogs. Link to individual posts on other blogs. Link to stories you are discussing. Link to Wikipedia.com. Link to posts you made in the past. Above all, link. The whole notion of the Internet is built on interconnections of shared information, so without links, all you have is unsubstantiated text. This would tend to isolate your work, when it could be out there making friends!

Participate

Once you've mastered posting and linking, the next thing to do is participate in the discussions going on around you. Bloggers love to get comments; comments let them know someone is out there reading, so share your opinions and thoughts as often as possible. The great thing about the blogosphere is that the text out there is usually joined by a handy "comment" button, giving you the power to turn that text into a conversation. So participate, participate, participate!

Blogging is Magic

Blogging is about power: the power of information. It isn't so different from magic, really. We use our will to help create and shape the reality we want. I urge everyone to use a ritual tool they may have never considered before, their computer.

The act of Pagan blogging is like the art of magic: a technology that can aid our communities in ways we never thought possible before. With these new tools we can shape what we may want as individuals and as communities; how we want to think, whom we want to trust, and where we want to go in the future. Now, instead of small isolated groups, our blog "spells" can involve our entire global religious community, and even other fellow travelers who have wisdom to share.

The Meddling Media
by Diana Rajchel

You might remember the television show *Charmed*. It was about three attractive female Witches who used magic to save the world while also struggling to have normal lives. The show had both positive and negative effects on the Wiccan community. Producers often purchased props for the show from Pagan/Wiccan vendors, but their presentation of "practitioner" Witches was often unflattering. Some episodes explored the reality of Wicca, but the fictional media's confused response to Wicca as a minority religion, and their representation of Wiccans as superstitious, provoked a mixed response to real Wicca from the show's audience.

The way in which the real media portrays Wiccans and Wicca can help or hurt, too. Learning to recognize the difference between fact and opinion, and knowing when you're being steered in a particular direction, can help you to decide whether or not you want to go in that direction.

Signs of Trouble Ahead

Discordians[1] call fear-manipulating words *fnords*. Use of well-placed adjectives, strategic quotes, and clichéd speech to convey an opinion under the guise of reporting facts is a tactic employed by skilled manipulators. Those exposed to manipulative media will come away from the experience feeling exactly how the creator wants. Use of media to influence opinion is prevalent and integral at least to the way we live in the United States; it also is a profound form of magic.

A mainstream reporter has the possibility of being educated; self-sensationalizing Wiccans and Pagans, not so much.

The next time you read the news, try this: Take a pen and make a hash mark on a piece of paper each time you encounter an adjective. Then, circle each adjective. Contemplate what types of emotions each word invokes. Star the adjectives used to communicate fear. You might see words and phrases such as *crisis, terrorism, danger, hurtful,* or *blasts.*

Even positive articles can manipulate emotion, and good comments in an article are still manipulation. Using the fnord exercise, you can protect yourself from overt manipulation, which leaves you in control of your own emotional response.

When reporters write about Wicca, they tend to use a lot of adjectives, and lace their writing with opinions. This hap-

---

1. Discordianism is a modern, chaos-based religion founded in either 1958 or 1959. It has been described as both an elaborate joke disguised as a religion, and as a religion disguised as an elaborate joke. http://en.wikipedia.org/wiki/Discordianism.

269

pens because Wicca and witchcraft trigger deep-seated, probably unconscious, responses in even level-headed reporters. Because of these issues, little digs creep their way into reporting.

My review of Wren's Nest[2] news archives unearthed hundreds of examples of this approach to reporting about Wicca. For example, reporter Tom Lochner of what is now the *Contra-Costa Times*, wrote the following about the suicide of a fourteen-year-old boy in December 1997:

> Some people saw Eli as a lost kid. Born into a spiritual group—some call it a cult—that split up when he was 9. Eli stayed out late, cut classes, allegedly took drugs, played vampire games, dabbled in witchcraft and often wore eye makeup, nail polish, fake fangs and occasionally a dress. "Ethereal" is the word a former teacher used to describe the boy who "appeared to float in and out of the class," his long blond hair and black leather coat trailing behind him. His body was found in the Bay near the Berkeley Marina on Sept. 24. His signature black coat, without which he rarely went out, has not been found. Elijah Louis Jacobs was 14. But some believe Eli's death was linked to the shadowy world of witchcraft, vampire games and late night performances of *Rocky* that he inhabited while he was alive. Eli's parents were members of a group of about 50 people inspired by the teachings of a turn-of-the century Russian mystic and philosopher.

Let's analyze Lochner's writing. Starting with: *"some people saw Eli as a lost kid,"* the writer infers fault with the parents. *"Born in a spiritual group—some call it a cult"* further manipulates the impression given. Writing that *"Eli stayed out late, cut classes, allegedly took drugs, played vampire games, dabbled in witchcraft and often wore eye makeup . . ."* prompted a negative response from most readers in the Contra-Costa area.

---

2. Please see www.witchvox.com.

Now, let's apply a little fnord to the text.

Some people saw Eli as a fnord kid. Born into
a spiritual group—some call it a fnord—that
split up when he was 9, Eli stayed out late, cut
classes, fnord took fnord, played fnord games,
fnord in fnord and often wore fnord fnord,
fnord, fnord, fake fnord and occasionally a
fnord. "Fnord" is the word a former teacher used
to describe the boy who "appeared to fnord in
and out of the class," his fnord fnord hair and
fnord fnord coat trailing behind him. His body
was found in the Bay near the Berkeley Marina
on Sept. 24. His signature fnord coat, without
which he rarely went out, has not been found.
Elijah Louis Jacobs was 14. But some believe Eli's
death was linked to the fnord world of fnord,
fnord games and late night performances of
"fnord" that he inhabited while he was alive.
Eli's parents were members of a group of about
50 people inspired by the teachings of a turn-of-
the century Russian mystic and philosopher.

As you can see, the passage is almost unreadable with
the manipulative language blocked. Arguably, even use of
Eli's first name beyond its first appearance with his last name
is manipulative. Associated Press style standards dictate that
when referring to a person in an article, all references after
the first identification should be by the last name. Using the
first name violates this standard, and also personalizes the
tragedy motif of the story since "first name basis" suggests
an emotional connection.

Publicity Nightmares

With the manipulative language blocked, the passage tells
a different story. It's still a tragedy, but not one that blames
role-playing games, the occult, or being a normal teenager.

Sometimes Wiccans hurt themselves through paranoia and misinformation—even when such information is well intentioned. While articles rife with manipulative language can frustrate the most ardent Pagan/Wiccan public relations representative, the self-sensationalizing Wiccan does much more damage to the entire cause. A mainstream reporter has the possibility of being educated; self-sensationalizing Wiccans and Pagans, not so much. In fact, they often know just enough of what they're doing to make a mess for others.

Minnesota had one such public Pagan in their midst. In January of 2006, one Jonathon Sharkey attempted to capital-ize on his Pagan and vampyric leanings to gain publicity for his gubernatorial candidacy.

Sharkey's personal identity has little or nothing to do with modern Paganism, even though he claimed to represent the "witches, pagans and vampyrs party," and pictures of himself in ritual garb appeared on his Web site. Sharkey overlooked that politics are not shared by virtue of practicing a religion; and he didn't seem to know the term "Pagan" can refer to literally hundreds of religions, and that "vampyr" is as lifestyle choice by a different subculture.

Sharkey created a stir among the neo-Pagan community in Minnesota, though, and many members put their face in palm and winced. Sharkey was a public relations Catch-22. The community's silence could be mistaken for agreement to the untruths he promoted, and if the community spoke out, more attention to Sharkey would feed the problem.

The media and those who work in it are neither enemies nor demonic entities.

Silence was the chosen path of action, and he has been heard from minimally since extradition to Indiana. Sharkey had skipped out on probation for two felony charges, one for stalking an ex-girlfriend (which Sharkey claims were spurious) and another for escaping imprisonment because he illegally left the state while he was out on bond. As of August 2, 2006, Sharkey was released from an Indiana prison and has returned to Minnesota. At the point this article is written, his political campaign stays quiet. In an interview given upon his release, Sharkey said "Witch hunts are alive and well!" No one commented on how his actions started that particular hunt.

Sometimes, in an effort to remain neutral, the story goes horribly awry as someone uses witchcraft as a shock tactic to draw attention to him/herself or a favorite cause.

The damage of people like Sharkey plays out in the presses, because the agents of the press are the agents of forming stereotypes. Stereotypes, like golems, require a grain of truth to sustain themselves. Those grains can be taken from Sharkey and others like him. Some editorialists have labeled Wiccans "silly," or as "fantasists." So long as these writers can demonstrate their opinion has foundation, such judgments are well within the limits of free press. The downside of freedom of speech, press, and thought is that all individuals have the right to write what they actually think about a given individual or group as long as it's strictly opinion or as long as it's true (but without the deliberate intent of causing damage).

Wiccans are not and should not be immune to public criticism. While no one likes being told they're wrong, learning to examine such comments before reacting will raise the public's opinion of Wiccans and other Pagans among academics, reporters, and marketers.

The media and those who work in it are neither enemies nor demonic entities. These writers are people, and it's a matter of pride to have a writer's voice shine through the work. Sometimes this comes out well, such as a positive article about a Pagan Pride celebration. Sometimes this comes out poorly, when the latest brutality to a cat becomes speculation on what those creepy Wiccans are doing. Sometimes, in an effort to remain neutral, the story goes horribly awry as someone uses witchcraft as a shock tactic to draw attention to him/herself or a favorite cause. A reporter who just doesn't know better is sucked in. The fnords are not out to get you. Use the magic founded in common sense. Speak clearly and intelligently, and the slow magical change of an improved realistic image of Wicca will manifest.

About the Authors

Parthena Black is an intuitive reader, creative artist, and owner of Oy! My Goddess! Creations. She is the editor of the Dreams site at BellaOnline, and active in the Pagan community in Tulsa, Oklahoma.

Dallas Jennifer Cobb lives in an enchanted waterfront village. She's freed up resources for what she loves: family, gardens, fitness, and fabulous food. When she's not running country roads or wandering the beach, she writes articles and a video documentary called "Disparate Places." Contact her at gaias.garden@sympatico.ca.

Raven Digitalis lives in Missoula, Montana. He is a student of anthropology, the author of the forthcoming book *Goth Craft* (Llewellyn Worldwide), and a third-year neo-Pagan priest. He lives with his priestess, both of whom hold community rituals, tarot readings, and co-operate the metaphysical supply business Twigs & Brews. In his spare time, he is a gothic-industrial radio and club DJ.

Taylor Ellwood is coauthor of *Creating Magickal Entities* (Egregore Publishing) and *Kink Magic* (Immanion Press). He is the author of *Pop Culture Magick* (Immanion Press), *Space/Time Magic* (Immanion Press), and *Inner Alchemy* (Immanion Press). He is the editor of *Magick on the Edge: Adventures in Experimental Magick,* an anthology from Immanion Press. For more information about Taylor, please visit http://www.thegreenwolf.com, or his blog at http://teriel.livejournal.com.

Emely Flak is a practicing solitary Witch from Daylesford, Australia. When she is not writing, she is at her day job as a learning and development professional. This busy mother of two and partner of one is also trained as a civil celebrant. Much of her work is dedicated to embracing the ancient wisdom of

Wicca for personal empowerment, particularly in the competitive work environment.

Link writes about how everyday life can be sacred and magical. He began learning about alternative religion, divination, and magic in the mid-1970s, and became active in the Craft in 1993; he is certified as clergy with both Covenant of the Goddess and ULC. His work has been published in the U.S., Canada, England, Ireland, Holland, and Australia. He enjoys good food, good wine, bad humor, camping, gardening, traveling, almost anything Brazilian, the ocean, sci-fi, and sleeping late at least once a week.

Luna holds a degree in psychology and has been a solitary Witch for over twenty years. She lives with her wonderful husband and their beautiful dog in Connecticut where she celebrates the turning of the wheel, gardening, writing, and making hand-crafted quilts and gifts for loved ones.

Lupa is a twenty-something Pagan and experimental magician who lives in Seattle with her husband and fellow author, Taylor Ellwood. A totemist and panentheist, she is the author of *Fang and Fur, Blood and Bone: A Primal Guide to Animal Magic* (Immanion Press, 2006) and the forthcoming *A Field Guide to Otherkin* (Immanion Press, 2007). She may be found at http://www.thegreenwolf.com.

Paniteowl lives in the foothills of the Appalachians in northeast Pennsylvania. She was raised in an eclectic family of spiritualists. Currently, she is building a spiritual retreat center on a plot of woodland and writing a book about the Pagan community.

Daniel Pharr grew up in the desert Southwest. He was introduced to the Pagan and ancient ways of the Goddess almost twenty years ago. He has studied reiki, reflexology, therapeutic touch, massage, tarot, astrology, intuitive counseling, and herbalism. Pharr is also a scuba instructor, a martial arts teacher with a black belt in Kenpo karate, and a certified fire-walker instructor.

Jason Pitzl-Waters is a writer, blogger, DJ, and amateur theologian. He currently maintains the The Wild Hunt weblog and hosts a Pagan and occult Internet radio show and podcast. Jason plans to return to college in 2007 to study religion.

Diana Rajchel lives in Minneapolis and writes about everything she possibly can. She has practiced Wicca for nine years and has believed in the magic of the divine for much longer. She actually can't stand long walks on the beach with another person, and never holds hands on ice.

SkyeWolf (a.k.a. Niki Browning) has been a practicing Pagan for over fifteen years. She currently works as a freelance artist and is the art director for a small online publishing house. She resides in her home in Connecticut with her husband, two children, nine cats, two dogs, and three frogs.

Tammy Sullivan is a full-time writer and solitary Witch who writes from her home in the foothills of the Great Smoky Mountains. She is the author of several books. Her work has appeared in the Llewellyn almanacs and *Circle* magazine.

Patricia Telesco considers herself a down-to-earth Kitchen Witch whose love of folklore and world-wide customs flavor every spell and ritual. Self-trained and self-initiated, she later received initiation into the Strega tradition of Italy. Her strongest beliefs lie in following personal vision, being tolerant of other traditions, making life an act of worship, and being creative so that magic grows with you. She lectures and workshops around the country, and she, or her writing, has appeared on TV segments including *Sightings* on muli-cultural divination systems and *National Geographic Today—Solstice Celebrations*. Telesco maintains a visible presence in metaphysical journals including *Circle Network News*, and on the Internet through popular sites like www.witchvox.com (festival focus). Her interactive home page is located at www.loresinger.com.

AarTiana has practiced many forms of natural spirituality since the early 1990s. She lives in western Montana with her husband, her two teenage children, and an old black tomcat with white whiskers named Chuckles. She is a professional astrologer, tarot card reader, dowser, and is currently changing her occupation to become a certified master herbalist. She somehow also manages to have an organic garden, crochet professionally, and is co-creating *Tië eldaliéva*, meaning the Elven Spiritual Path. Find out more by visiting http://www.myspace.com/aartiana.

Annie Wilder was raised Catholic in a family that had strong intuitive abilities, and the unseen world of angels, spirits, and lost souls has always been a part of her everyday life. Wilder holds a Level II certification in reiki, and is the author of *House of Spirits and Whispers: The True Story of a Haunted House*. She still lives in the haunted house where her story takes place.

Lady Mandrake Windwillow is a Pagan priestess living in York County, Pennsylvania, with her husband and three children. She has been a practicing Pagan since 1995, and is very active in the local Pagan community. She is an eclectic Kitchen Witch who enjoys cooking, crafts, and sewing. She is head of Morning Mist Grove, a local solitary support group, and is currently working with other local Pagan clergy in forming Spirit Calling, a Pagan umbrella organization for small Pagan groups and individuals.

Notes

Notes

Notes

Notes

Notes

Notes

Notes

Notes

Notes